COMMUNICATION SKILLS
virtual training

ATD Workshop Series

COMMUNICATION SKILLS
virtual training

MAUREEN OREY

PRESS

Alexandria, Virginia

ATD Press is an internationally renowned source of insightful and practical information on talent development, training, and professional development.

ATD Press
1640 King Street
Alexandria, VA 22314 USA

Ordering information: Books published by ATD Press can be purchased by visiting ATD's website at td.org/books or by calling 800.628.2783 or 703.683.8100.

Library of Congress Control Number: 2020951575

ISBN-10: 1-952157-71-4
ISBN-13: 978-1-952157-71-4
e-ISBN: 978-1-952157-72-1

ATD Press Editorial Staff
Director: Sarah Halgas
Manager: Melissa Jones
Content Manager, Learning and Development: Eliza Blanchard
Text Design: Ana Ilieva (Foreman/Design) and Rosemary Aguilar Mingo (ATD Press)
Cover Design: Rose Richey
Presentation Slide and Handout Art: Shutterstock and Canstockphoto

Printed by BR Printers, San Jose, CA

Contents

SECTION II: ESSENTIALS OF EFFECTIVE COMMUNICATION SKILLS TRAINING 94

The ATD Workshop Series

 **Association for Talent Development**

Whether you are a professional trainer who needs to pull together a new training program next week, or someone who does a bit of training as a part of your job, you'll find the ATD Workshop Series is a timesaver.

Topics deliver key learning on today's most pressing business needs, including training for communication skills, leadership, coaching, new supervisors, customer service, new employee orientation, and more. The series is designed for busy training and HR professionals, consultants, and managers who need to deliver training quickly to optimize performance now.

Each ATD Workshop book provides all the content and trainer's tools you need to create and deliver compelling training guaranteed to

- **Enhance** learner engagement.
- **Deepen** learner understanding.
- **Increase** learning application.

Each book in the series offers innovative and engaging programs designed by leading experts and grounded in design and delivery best practices and theory. It is like having an expert trainer helping you with each step in the workshop process. The straightforward, practical instructions help you prepare and deliver the workshops quickly and effectively. Flexible timing options allow you to choose from half-day, full-day, and two-day workshop formats, or to create your own, using the tips and strategies presented for customizing the workshops to fit your unique business environment. Each ATD Workshop book also comes with access to all the training materials you will need, including activities, handouts, tools, assessments, and PowerPoint slides.

At ATD we're dedicated to creating a world that works better and empowering professionals like you to develop talent in the workplace. We hope the ATD Workshop Series adds value to your work.

Preface

Everyone has something to say, but not everyone communicates well. In today's virtual world, clear and concise communication that gets your message across clearly and completely is essential to your continued success.

Whether you are a good speaker or not, every person has a message that should be communicated and heard. Learning to communicate your message is much more challenging than it may seem. It takes self-reflection to discover your voice, and it takes courage and skill to use it.

Communication affects almost every part of the workplace—it can help us improve relationships and increase performance, or it can reduce trust, damage relationships, and ultimately lead to the failure of projects, teams, and organizations. Improving your communication skills takes the willingness to assess yourself honestly and the courage to take action and change existing behaviors that do not enhance communication or build relationships.

Teaching others to have better communication skills is very rewarding and can even change lives! I once had a participant come to me a few months after attending a workshop on effective communication skills; she attended the workshop because she was struggling to communicate effectively with her boss. Then she shared with me how she implemented the new skills learned in the workshop, and as a result the relationship with her boss had improved and led to positive progress in her career growth! How cool is that?

As a facilitator, you too can enable others to gain valuable skills and grow personally. If you are a seasoned trainer, you are likely already using many of these designs and formats. You may not be an expert on training or communication yet; however, with the tools and resources in this book, you can help people strengthen their communication skills. The agendas and supplemental materials included here will provide all the tools you need to deliver programs that will improve communication skills for individuals, teams, and organizations. It is exciting work that can change lives and improve organizational results.

Maureen Orey, CPTD
San Diego, California
January 2021

Introduction

How to Use This Book

What's in This Chapter

- Why communication skills matter
- What you need to know about training
- Estimates of time required
- A broad overview of what the book includes

Why Do Communication Skills Matter?

In this world of constant change, effective communication is a crucial skill set for leaders and individual contributors. Communication is the key to both success and failure—making or breaking relationships, teams, or organizations. Poor communication reduces productivity, trust, and morale, whereas positive and respectful communication builds relationships and collaboration and increases productivity.

Verbal and nonverbal communication and attentive listening skills are valuable in the workplace. Good communication skills go beyond simply talking and conversations; communicating well in written reports, email, and in virtual settings (such as WebEx, Zoom, or Microsoft Teams) is also essential. Workplace communication can be a challenging and difficult task. It takes a strong sense of self, emotional control, and personal confidence to allow yourself to become vulnerable with your colleagues. But without strong communication skills, developing successful working relationships is nearly impossible.

Communication is the vehicle for sharing information with colleagues; it is at the heart of team building, customer service, conflict management, and every other interaction in the workplace.

The goal of all communication is to develop a common understanding of what was said and to ensure the message that comes across is the same to all parties involved.

Understanding the benefits of effective communication helps companies focus on developing a workforce that can communicate with one another as well as with customers, vendors, and business partners. If you are searching to build a positive, collaborative, and trusting work environment, good communication skills must be your foundation.

The first edition of this book in 2004 approached the topic of communication skills somewhat differently, covering a wide variety of topics, with each topic presented at a very high level. This edition offers a new approach. Fewer topics are covered overall, but each topic—listening skills, business writing, communicating your message, and verbal and nonverbal communication—is explored more deeply. In fact, each topic can stand alone as its own half-day workshop. We've also updated the content to address communication skills training in the virtual space.

Providing your participants with a deeper, more nuanced understanding of communication will give them a solid foundation upon which to build strong skills and relationships in the workplace. The content, activities, and tools offered here are designed to help you to start this critical learning immediately

What Do I Need to Know About Training?

The ATD Workshop series is designed to be adaptable for many levels of both training facilitation and topic expertise. Circle the answers in the following chart that most closely align with your levels of expertise and your organization's commitment to learning.

QUICK ASSESSMENT: HOW EXPERT DO I NEED TO BE?			
Question	3	2	1
What is your expertise as a facilitator?	Expert (more than 5 years, always awesome evaluations)	Some experience (1–5 years, sometimes talk too much)	Beginner (less than 1 year, no idea what to do)
How familiar are you with the topic?	Evolving expert (have taken courses, read books, created materials, and it)	Some experience (have taken courses, read books, created materials)	Beginner (had a course in school)
How committed is your company to investing in training or performance improvement?	Integral part of our corporate culture	Depends on the topic—this one is hot right now	They want it cheap and fast
TOTAL:			

Now calculate your score. Each circled answer from column 3 gets three points, column 2 gets two points, and column 1 gets one point.

If you scored 1–3: You're likely a novice at both training and this topic. Your best bet is to stick as closely as possible to the materials as they are. Spend extra time with the content to learn as much as you can about it. Also, closely read chapter 7 on training delivery and consider practicing with a colleague before delivering the program.

If you scored 4–6: You may be a topic expert. Use the outline and materials, and feel free to include materials you have developed and believe are relevant to the topic.

If you scored 7–9: You're a training expert. Feel free to adapt the agendas and materials as you see fit and use any materials that you have already developed, or simply incorporate training activities, tools, handouts, and so forth into your own agenda.

For more on facilitation skills, see chapter 7. Chapter 11 also includes a comprehensive assessment instrument that will help you manage your professional development and increase the effectiveness of your communication skills training sessions (see Assessment 4: Facilitator Competencies).

What Considerations Need to Be Addressed in a Virtual Delivery Model?

Despite the many advantages to virtual training (such as reduced travel and facility expenses and increased scheduling flexibility), the modality does come with some potential pitfalls. You will be best positioned to maximize the benefits and minimize the hazards by taking the time to address these concerns. Some items to think about and plan for in advance of a virtual session include:

- Ensure you have adequately prepared the content and practiced using any online tools needed in the session. Can you set up breakout rooms and move back and forth between them and the main session? Do you know how to mute and unmute participants as a group and individually?
- Organize the distribution of any materials as needed during the session. Will you send them by email or through file share? Create your plan and communicate it to your participants.

- Make sure participants understand their role in making a virtual training successful. Emphasize the necessity for active participation. Ensure that participants know how to use the platform's interactivity tools. Be sure to vary the methodology of instruction every eight to 10 minutes if possible (for example with lectures, activities, worksheets, breakout sessions, large group discussions, or Q&As).

- Remember that your participants are sitting in front of their screens for extended periods of time. Try to stick to scheduled breaks and encourage participants to move away from their computers during these breaks—this will help them better focus during the session. To avoid potential environmental distractions during the session, encourage participants to close other activities or applications (such as email and other chat programs) and put away their mobile devices.

How Much Time Will Preparation Take?

Putting together and facilitating a face-to-face training workshop, even when the agendas, activities, tools, and assessments are created for you, can be time consuming. Adding the element of a virtual environment contributes to the need to thoroughly prepare and plan. You will have to be comfortable not only with the content, but also with the platform being used, potential connectivity and functionality challenges and their solutions, and effective ways to get and keep participants engaged with you, each other, and the content. For planning purposes, estimate four to five days of preparation time for a two-day virtual workshop.

What Are the Important Features of the Book?

Section I includes the various workshop designs (from a half day to two days) with agendas and thumbnails from PowerPoint slides as well as a chapter on customizing the workshop for your circumstances. The chapters included are:

- Chapter 1. Two-Day Workshop (15 hours program time) + Agenda + PPT (thumbnails)
- Chapter 2. One-Day Workshop (7.5 hours program time) + Agenda + PPT (thumbnails)
- Chapter 3. Half-Day Workshop (3 to 4 hours program time) + Agenda + PPT (thumbnails)
- Chapter 4. Customizing the Communication Skills Workshop

The workshop chapters include advice, instructions, workshop at-a-glance tables, and full program agendas.

Section II is standard from book to book in the ATD Workshop Series as a way to provide a consistent foundation of training principles. This section's chapters follow the ADDIE model—the classic instructional design model named after its steps (analysis, design, development, implementation, and evaluation). The chapters are based on best practices and crafted with input from experienced training practitioners. They are meant to help you get up to speed as quickly as possible. Each chapter includes several additional recurring features to help you understand the concepts and ideas presented. The **Bare Minimum** gives you the bare bones of what you need to know about the topic. **Key Points** summarize the most important points of each chapter. **What to Do Next** guides you to your next action steps. And, finally, the **Additional Resources** section at the end of each chapter gives you options for further reading to broaden your understanding of training design and delivery. Section II chapters include:

- Chapter 5. Identifying Needs for Communication Skills Virtual Training
- Chapter 6. Understanding the Foundations of Training Design
- Chapter 7. Delivering Your Communication Skills Workshop: Be a Great Facilitator
- Chapter 8. Evaluating Workshop Results

Section III covers information about post-workshop learning:

- Chapter 9. The Follow-Up Coach

Section IV includes all the supporting documents and online guidance:

- Chapter 10. Learning Activities
- Chapter 11. Assessments
- Chapter 12. Handouts
- Chapter 13. Online Tools and Downloads

The book includes everything you need to prepare for and deliver your communication skills workshop:

- **Agendas,** the heart of the series, are laid out in three columns for ease of delivery. The first column shows the timing, the second gives the presentation slide number and image for quick reference, and the third gives instructions and facilitation notes. These are designed to be straightforward, simple agendas that you can take into the training room and use to stay on track. They also include cues on the learning activities, notes about tools or handouts to include, and other important delivery tips. You can download the agendas from the website (see chapter 13) and print them out for easy use.

- **Learning activities,** which are more detailed than the agendas, cover the objectives of the activity, the time and materials required, the steps involved, variations on the activity in some cases, and wrap-up or debriefing questions or comments.

- **Assessments, handouts, and tools** are the training materials you will provide to learners to support the training program. These can include scorecards for games, instructions, reference materials, samples, or self-assessments.

- **Presentation media** (PowerPoint slides) are deliberately designed to be simple so you can customize them for your company and context. They are provided for your convenience.

All the program materials are available for download, customization, and duplication. See chapter 13 for instructions on how to access the materials.

How Are the Agendas Laid Out?

The following agenda is a sample from the two-day communication skills workshop.

Two-Day Workshop Agenda

Day 1: (8 a.m. to 4 p.m.)

TIMING	SLIDES	ACTIVITIES/NOTES/CONSIDERATIONS
8 a.m. (10 min)	Slide 1 ATD Workshop Effective Communication Skills	**Welcome and Introduction** Briefly welcome the participants and introduce yourself. Give them a brief overview of the functionality or interactivity that will be used during the session (such as polls, chat, whiteboard, and breakout sessions). A sample functionality overview has been provided to you. This sample is specific to the WebEx environment. Ensure that participants are aware that they may be asked to share their screens or cameras as part of the exercises and activities during the workshop.

TIMING	SLIDES	ACTIVITIES/NOTES/CONSIDERATIONS
8:10 a.m. (15 min)	Slide 2 Two-Day Workshop Objectives • Identify the most common barriers of communication. • Explain the Five Cs of Effective Communication. • Assess your listening skills. • Explain and practice active listening skills. • Determine the best way to get your point across. • Examine situational dynamics to assess the best approach for communicating in challenging situations. • Apply effective principles for face-to-face, written, and virtual scenarios.	**Learning Activity 1: Objective Decision** • **Handout 1a: Objective Decision** • **Poll: Objectives** This activity provides an innovative way to facilitate the discussion about session objectives rather than simply reading them to the participants. Ask participants to follow the instructions in the handout. When they are finished ask them to select the objective in the poll that corresponds to the one they highlighted. Share poll results with all.
8:25 a.m. (10 min)	Slide 3 Ground Rules and Expectations • Participate! • Explore new ideas • Have fun • "Vegas rule" • What else?	**Ground Rules and Expectations** Facilitate the discussion about ground rules and expectations for the course. Adjust times for starting, breaks, and lunches as needed to accommodate your environmental factors. It is important to establish a positive learning environment. Ask participants to give you a green check if they are in agreement with the ground rules for the session.
8:35 a.m. (15 min)	**Whiteboard:** Who is the most difficult person in the world? Four Corners: When do you have the most energy? Morning? | Afternoon? All Day? | Night? In four corners of the room, meet to discuss ... Who is the most difficult person to communicate with, and why?	**Learning Activity 2: The Most Difficult Person** • **Handout 2: The Most Difficult Person in the World** Get participants thinking by using Handout 2. Debrief the questions using any method you wish (for example, the chat pane or raise hand). Capture responses on the whiteboard so all can see.

How Do I Use This Book?

If you've ever read a Choose Your Own Adventure book, you will recognize that this book follows a similar principle. Think back to the self-assessment at the beginning of this introduction:

- If you chose training expert, you can get right to work preparing one of the workshops in Section I. Use Section II as a reference. Each chapter features a sidebar or other information written by the author, who has much experience in the topic under consideration. This advice can help guide your preparation, delivery, and evaluation of training.

- If you chose topic expert, read Section II in depth, and skim the topic content.

- If you chose novice at training and the topic, then spend some serious time familiarizing yourself with both Sections I and II.

Once you have a general sense of the material, assemble your workshop. Select the appropriate agenda and then modify the times and training activities as needed and desired. Assemble the materials and familiarize yourself with the topic, the activities, and presentation media.

Key Points

- Oral and written communication skills are essential to individual and organizational success.

- Effective listening skills help build positive relationships.

- The workshops in this book are designed to be effective at all levels of trainer expertise.

- Good training requires an investment of time.

- The book contains everything you need to create a workshop, including agendas, learning activities, presentation media, assessments, handouts, and tools.

What to Do Next

- Make yourself familiar with the functionality, both as a facilitator and as a participant, of the platform that you will use to host the training program.

- Review the agendas presented in Section I and select the best fit for your requirements, time constraints, and budget.

- Based on your level of expertise, skim or read in-depth the chapters in Section II.

- Consider what kind of follow-up learning activities you will want to include with the workshop by reviewing Section III.

Additional Resources

Biech, E. (2008). *10 Steps to Successful Training.* Alexandria, VA: ASTD Press.

Biech, E., ed. (2014). *ASTD Handbook: The Definitive Reference for Training & Development*, 2nd edition. Alexandria, VA: ASTD Press.

Emerson, T., and M. Stewart. (2011). *The Learning and Development Book.* Alexandria, VA: ASTD Press.

McCain, D.V., and D.D. Tobey. (2004). *Facilitation Basics.* Alexandria, VA: ASTD Press.

Piskurich, G. (2003). *Trainer Basics.* Alexandria, VA: ASTD Press.

Stolovitch, H.D., and E.J. Keeps. (2011). *Telling Ain't Training*, 2nd edition. Alexandria, VA: ASTD Press.

SECTION I

The Workshops

Chapter 1

Two-Day Communication Skills Workshop

What's in This Chapter

- Objectives of the two-day communication skills workshop
- Summary chart for the flow of content and activities
- Two-day program agenda

Whether you choose a two-day, one-day, half-day, or custom workshop format, time spent on developing communication skills will bring solid results in personal and organizational performance. There are, however, a number of benefits in conducting longer workshops. In two days, participants get to know each other, build rapport, delve deeper into a topic, practice the skills they are learning, and discuss and reflect on the application and relevance to workplace scenarios.

A well-designed workshop anticipates the natural and predictable "low energy" times during the day. It is essential to incorporate activities that engage participants, getting them out of their lull and taking part in relevant and meaningful activities, small group discussion, and practice.

Facilitating a two-day (or longer) workshop requires the facilitator to have a high level of energy, focus, and a keen ability to read the energy level of the participants throughout the duration of the program. A great way to keep the participants engaged and the energy high is to manage the flow of activities, presentations, and small- or large-group discussions. Just like frequency of commercial breaks on televised programs, consider changing your training method every 10 to 15 minutes.

This chapter provides a comprehensive two-day workshop agenda using the principles of active training. It is designed to keep the content relevant, meaningful, and interactive. Day one focuses on oral communication and how to listen and deliver your message effectively. Day two focuses on effective written communication and the strategies for getting your message across in writing.

Two-Day Workshop Objectives

By the end of the two-day workshop, participants will be able to:

- Identify the most common barriers for communication.
- Explain the Five Cs of Effective Communication.
- Assess their personal listening skills.
- Explain and practice active listening skills.
- Determine the best way to get their point across.
- Examine situational dynamics to assess the best approach for communicating in challenging situations.
- Apply effective principles for face-to-face, written, and virtual scenarios.

Two-Day Workshop Overview

Day 1 Overview

TOPICS	TIMING
Welcome and Introduction	10 minutes
Learning Activity 1. Objective Decision	15 minutes
Ground Rules and Expectations	10 minutes
Learning Activity 2. The Most Difficult Person	15 minutes
Communication Model Process	10 minutes
BREAK	**10 minutes**
Learning Activity 3. Identify the Noise	10 minutes
The Communication Pie (Three Modes of Communication)	10 minutes
Congruent Communication	5 minutes
Incongruent Communication	5 minutes
Vocal Tone and Word Emphasis	10 minutes
The Role of Emotion in Communication	5 minutes
Discussion and Brainstorm: Symptoms of Fear and Anger	15 minutes
The Emotional and Rational Brain	5 minutes
BREAK	**10 minutes**

TOPICS	TIMING
Emotional Hijacking and the Reptilian Brain	5 minutes
Strategies for Gaining Emotional Control	15 minutes
Indicators of Relaxation	10 minutes
Managing the Emotion	5 minutes
Communication Awareness Model	10 minutes
BREAK	**10 minutes**
Learning Activity 5. Surgical Analysis of Your Story	35 minutes
Five Steps to Effective Communication	15 minutes
Morning Debrief	10 minutes
LUNCH	**60 minutes**
Assessment 1. Listening Behavior Assessment	15 minutes
Learning Activity 6. Listening Is More Than Hearing	30 minutes
Basic Listening	5 minutes
BREAK	**10 minutes**
Learning Activity 7. The Listening Stick (Part 1)	15 minutes
Principles of Active Listening (Part 1)	15 minutes
Principles of Active Listening (Part 2)	15 minutes
BREAK	**10 minutes**
Small-Group Brainstorm: Barriers to Listening	15 minutes
Reflection and Action Plan	10 minutes
Day 1 Summary	10 minutes
Final Q&A, Homework, Day 2 Reminders, and Informal Evaluations	10 minutes
TOTAL	**480 minutes (8 Hours)**

Day 2 Overview

TOPICS	TIMING
Welcome and Reconnect	10 minutes
Revisit Ground Rules and Expectations	15 minutes
Learning Activity 9. Alpha Beta Exercise	50 minutes
Activity Debrief: Alpha Beta Exercise	10 minutes
BREAK	**10 minutes**
Whiteboard: What Makes Good Business Writing?	5 minutes
Model for Effective Business Writing	10 minutes
Planning Your Writing Content	15 minutes
Whiteboard: Mind Map	5 minutes
Learning Activity 11. Document Planning Mind Map	15 minutes

Day 2 Overview (cont.)

TOPICS	TIMING
BREAK	**10 minutes**
Brainstorm . . . Brainstorming!	10 minutes
Five Cs of Effective Communication	5 minutes
Learning Activity 12. Five Cs	15 minutes
Learning Activity 13. Clear Communication	25 minutes
Learning Activity 14. Concise Communication	15 minutes
Learning Activity 15. Complete Communication	15 minutes
LUNCH	**60 minutes**
Learning Activity 16. Correct Communication	20 minutes
Learning Activity 17. Considerate Communication: Circles of Influence	20 minutes
BREAK	**15 minutes**
Learning Activity 18. Identify Your Reader's Needs	20 minutes
Learning Activity 19. Draft Your Message	30 minutes
Most Commonly Forgotten Communication Factors	10 minutes
BREAK	**10 minutes**
Design the Document	10 minutes
Reflection and Action Plan	15 minutes
Day 2 Summary	15 minutes
Final Q&A and Evaluation	15 minutes
TOTAL	**480 minutes (8 Hours)**

Considerations for the Virtual Environment

Conducting a workshop in a virtual format is often necessary to provide the benefits of time and location flexibility as well as to account for cost. Unfortunately, this modality also brings the risk of some challenges, such as technology limitations, distracted learners, a lack of non-verbal cues, and the highly beneficial informal, but relevant, sidebar conversations that take place among learners in a shared space with a shared interest. When considering conducting a workshop in a virtual format, the following recommendations may help minimize some of these risks:

- Consider breaking up the content into smaller chunks. Ideally, virtual sessions should be no longer than two to four hours a day. See chapter 4 for suggestions on how this content can be grouped into shorter or topic-specific sessions.

- To keep participants engaged, ensure that you maintain a high level of energy and frequently solicit input, both verbal and through the use of the technology tools throughout the duration of the workshop.

- Actively seek frequent feedback from participants to gauge their understanding.
- Use the video feature as much as possible so participants can see that they have an instructor who is working with them and not just sharing static slides on a screen.
- Encourage participants to use their video features when speaking to help better engage with one another.

Preparation

While all facilitation sessions require preparation, the success of a virtual session is even more dependent on how carefully the facilitator prepares and the completion of a thorough and deliberate setup. The following checklists have been provided to help you ensure a smooth and effective workshop delivery. Please note, these checklists have been created with a WebEx environment in mind. As technologies and platforms can differ, you are encouraged to modify these recommendations based on the specific needs of your delivery.

Pre-Workshop—Facilitator Checklist

✓	TASK	SUGGESTED TIMEFRAME
	Upload the presentation files.	One week prior to the first session.
	Review the facilitator guide and any other course materials.	Ideally, one week prior to the start of the first session, but no later than 72 hours in advance.
	Validate the final participant list.	Ideally, one week prior to the start of the first session, but no later than 72 hours in advance.
	Send a welcome email to participants. Let them know you are looking forward to the class, and include reminders to complete any necessary prework and to verify connection and compatibility. Highlight the fact that this is designed to be an interactive workshop, which means that they may be asked to share their screen and video camera during the sessions, so they may want to ensure appropriate and respectful appearance and attire. In addition, they will be asked to interact with others in the session frequently and will need to minimize any external distractions to get the most favorable learning experience from the course.	One week prior to the first session.
	Create polls and breakout rooms.	At least 72 hours before the first session.

Pre-Workshop—Facilitator Checklist (cont.)

✓	TASK	SUGGESTED TIMEFRAME
	Ensure you're familiar with how the interactivity functionality within your presentation platform works. You need to be able to explain this to participants. You may also want to create a short cheat sheet that you can use to demonstrate these functions as you welcome participants to the session. This is particularly important if you are conducting a session for participants from multiple organizations.	At least 72 hours before the first session.

Create Polls

Create these polls before the start of Day 1 of the workshop. Ensure that each poll is set to share responses with all participants.

✓	LOCATION	POLL RESPONSES
	Slide 2 (Objectives)	• Identify the most common barriers of communication. • Explain the Five Cs of Effective Communication. • Assess your listening skills. • Explain and practice active listening skills. • Determine the best way to get your point across. • Examine situational dynamics to assess the best approach for communicating in challenging situations. • Apply effective principles for face-to-face, written, and virtual scenarios.
	Before Slide 7 (Communication Pie)	• Words we use • How we say words, tone of voice, style • Facial expression, body language

Create Breakout Rooms

The following breakout rooms will need to be created before the start of the workshop. Create a list of who has been assigned to each room that you can display onscreen at the start of the activity.

✓	ROOM DESCRIPTION	NOTES
	Create enough breakout rooms that the participants can be split into groups of five or fewer. Randomly assign each participant to a room so that the groups are roughly equal in number. Label rooms: • Room 1 • Room 2 • Room 3 • Room 4 • and so on	You will use these breakout rooms for the following activities: • Learning Activity 3. Identify the Noise • Learning Activity 5. Surgical Analysis of Your Story • Barriers to Listening • Brainstorm . . . Brainstorming! • Learning Activity 18. Identify Your Reader's Needs
	Create four breakout rooms and randomly assign each person to one. Label rooms: • Winter • Spring • Summer • Fall	You will use these breakout rooms for the following activity: • Learning Activity 12. The Five Cs
	Create enough breakout rooms to accommodate breaking the group up into pairs. For example, if you have 20 participants, you will need 10 breakout rooms. Randomly assign each participant to a room. Label rooms: • Pair 1 • Pair 2 • Pair 3 • Pair 4 • and so on	You will use these breakout rooms for the following activities: • Learning Activity 7. Listening Stick (Part 1) • Learning Activity 13. Clear Communication • Learning Activity 14. Concise Communication • Learning Activity 15. Complete Communication • Learning Activity 16. Correct Communication • Learning Activity 19. Draft Your Message

Two-Day Workshop Agenda: Day 1

Day 1—Facilitator Checklist

✓	TASK	SUGGESTED TIMEFRAME
	Log into the workshop a minimum of 30 minutes prior to start of session to verify that the content is loaded and working as planned. Ensure that you have a printed copy of this guide in front of you.	Day of session.
	Verify breakout rooms and participant assignments.	Day of session.
	Ensure the desired settings are enabled for the presentation and participants.	Day of session.
	As an audio check and to verify that participants are able to interact as planned, greet each participant verbally as they enter and ask them to write their first name and hometown on the whiteboard.	Start 15 minutes before the presentation begins. This serves as an initial audio and connectivity check for the annotation and interactivity tools.

Agenda

Day 1 (8 a.m. to 4 p.m.)

TIMING	SLIDES	ACTIVITIES/NOTES/CONSIDERATIONS
8 a.m. (10 min)	Slide 1 ATD Workshop Effective Communication Skills	**Welcome and Introduction** Briefly welcome the participants and introduce yourself. Provide a quick overview of the functionality and interactivity elements that will be used during the session (e.g., polls, chat, whiteboard, breakout sessions). A sample functionality overview has been provided. This sample is specific to the WebEx environment. Ensure that participants are aware that they may be asked to share their screens or cameras as part of the exercises and activities during the workshop.

TIMING	SLIDES	ACTIVITIES/NOTES/CONSIDERATIONS
8:10 a.m. (15 min)	Slide 2 **Two-Day Workshop Objectives** - Identify the most common barriers of communication. - Explain the five Cs of effective communication. - Assess your listening skills. - Explain and practice active listening skills. - Determine the best way to get your point across. - Examine situational dynamics to assess the best approach for communicating in challenging situations. - Apply effective principles for face-to-face, written and virtual scenarios.	**Learning Activity 1. Objective Decision** - **Handout 1a. Objective Decision** - **Poll: Objectives** This activity provides an innovative way to facilitate the discussion about session objectives rather than simply reading them to the participants. Ask participants to follow the instructions in the handout. When they are finished ask them to use the poll to select the objective that corresponds to the one they highlighted. Share poll results with all.
8:25 a.m. (10 min)	Slide 3 **Ground Rules and Expectations** - Participate! - Explore new ideas - Have fun - "Vegas rule" - What else?	**Ground Rules and Expectations** Facilitate a discussion about ground rules and expectations for the course. Adjust times as needed for starting, breaks, and lunches. It is important to establish a positive learning environment. Ask participants to give you a green check if they are in agreement with the ground rules for the session.
8:35 a.m. (15 min)	Slide 4 **Whiteboard:** Who is the most difficult person in the world?	**Learning Activity 2. The Most Difficult Person** - **Handout 2. The Most Difficult Person in the World** Get participants thinking by using Handout 2. Debrief the questions using any method you wish (e.g., chat pane or raise hand). Capture responses on the whiteboard so that all can see.
8:50 a.m. (10 min)	Slide 5 **Communication Process** Me — My Message — NOISE — My Message — You — Interpreter/Decoder Feedback: My clouded perception of your message to me	**Communication Model Process** Present the diagram of the communication process on Slide 5. Explain the process of miscommunication and how noise—real and perceived—can influence the communication process.

TIMING	SLIDES	ACTIVITIES/NOTES/CONSIDERATIONS
9 a.m. (10 min)	Slide 6 10-Minute Break	**BREAK** Encourage participants to get up and move around. Emphasize that they should try to look away from their computers or phones during the break if possible.
9:10 a.m. (10 min)	Slide 7 Identify the Noise EXTERNAL NOISE! INTERNAL NOISE?	**Learning Activity 3. Identify the Noise** • **Handout 3. Causes of Miscommunication** • **Breakout Room** **Direct participants to Handout 3.** Inform participants that they have been randomly broken into small groups for this learning activity. Show the list of participant assignments on the screen. Instruct participants to work together to identify and discuss the sources of noise that create miscommunication. **Give the groups 5–7 minutes to complete the handout.** Bring everyone back to the main room and debrief the questions using any method you wish (e.g., chat pane or raise hand). Capture ideas on the whiteboard.
	Slide 8 Poll Rank the importance of three aspects of communication: • Words we use • How we say words (tone of voice and style) • Facial expression and body language	**Poll** Ask participants to rank the importance of three aspects of communication: • **Words we use** • **How we say words (tone of voice and style)** • **Facial expression and body language** Share the poll results and introduce the next slide.

TIMING	SLIDES	ACTIVITIES/NOTES/CONSIDERATIONS
9:20 a.m. (10 min)	Slide 9 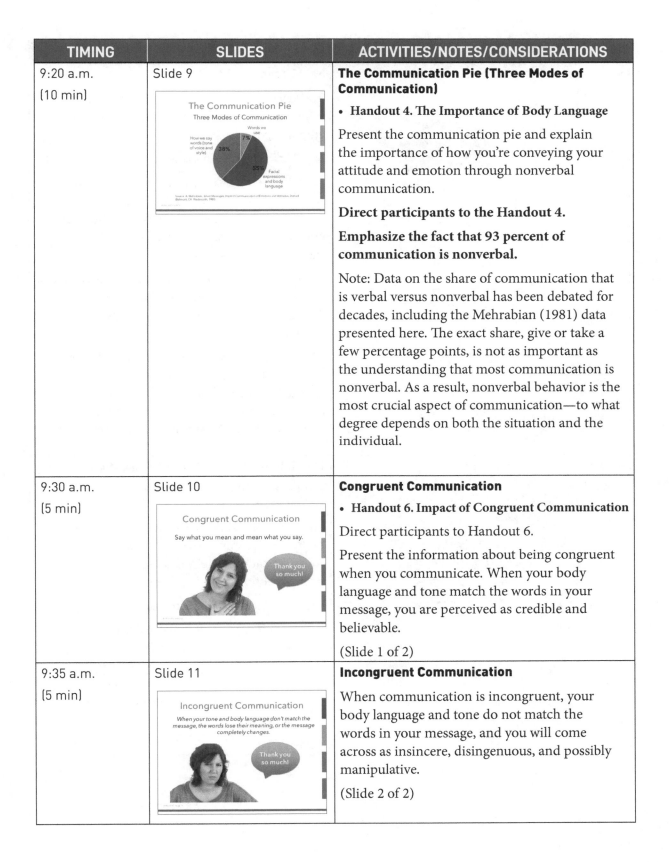	**The Communication Pie (Three Modes of Communication)** • **Handout 4. The Importance of Body Language** Present the communication pie and explain the importance of how you're conveying your attitude and emotion through nonverbal communication. **Direct participants to the Handout 4.** **Emphasize the fact that 93 percent of communication is nonverbal.** Note: Data on the share of communication that is verbal versus nonverbal has been debated for decades, including the Mehrabian (1981) data presented here. The exact share, give or take a few percentage points, is not as important as the understanding that most communication is nonverbal. As a result, nonverbal behavior is the most crucial aspect of communication—to what degree depends on both the situation and the individual.
9:30 a.m. (5 min)	Slide 10	**Congruent Communication** • **Handout 6. Impact of Congruent Communication** Direct participants to Handout 6. Present the information about being congruent when you communicate. When your body language and tone match the words in your message, you are perceived as credible and believable. (Slide 1 of 2)
9:35 a.m. (5 min)	Slide 11	**Incongruent Communication** When communication is incongruent, your body language and tone do not match the words in your message, and you will come across as insincere, disingenuous, and possibly manipulative. (Slide 2 of 2)

TIMING	SLIDES	ACTIVITIES/NOTES/CONSIDERATIONS
9:40 a.m. (10 min)	Slide 12 I didn't steal your cow yesterday.	**Vocal Tone and Word Emphasis** The key point here is that your words send different messages depending on the tone and emphasis you use. Say, "*I didn't steal your cow yesterday,*" six times. Each time emphasize a different word (*I, didn't, steal, your, cow,* and *yesterday*) and see how the meaning changes. For example, when you emphasize "I," it can sound as if you didn't steal the cow, but you know who did. To create class interaction, ask different participants to say the sentence while emphasizing a different word. Use the raise hand feature to ask for volunteers. This is a great place to point out how being in a virtual setting can influence the way a message is heard by the audience. This is especially true if you're not using a camera because the audience doesn't have the benefit of seeing any nonverbal cues.
9:50 a.m. (5 min)	Slide 13 The Role of Emotion in Communication	**The Role of Emotion in Communication** - **Handout 7. The Role of Emotion in Communication** This transition slide helps you shift the focus to the relationship between emotion and communication. Briefly discuss how quickly strong emotions can derail communication. Direct participants to Handout 7. Ask participants if they have experienced a situation where emotions derailed communication. Use a green check for yes and red X for no. Ask participants to raise their hand to share their experiences. Perhaps even tell a story about when this happened to you. (Slide 1 of 8)

TIMING	SLIDES	ACTIVITIES/NOTES/CONSIDERATIONS
9:55 a.m. (15 min)	Slide 14 Symptoms of Fear or Anger Adrenaline Fight or Flight Response	**Discussion and Brainstorm: Symptoms of Fear and Anger** Lead a brief, large-group brainstorming session to identify the symptoms of fear and anger. Explain that when you're angry or scared your fight-or-flight response kicks in, flooding your body with adrenaline. Your body responds accordingly: increasing your heart rate, blood pressure, anxiety, and breathing. The increased blood flow is directed to the big muscle groups in preparation for the fight, flight, or freeze response. The end result of this reaction is that your brain has less oxygen to use, and you cannot think as clearly in this emotional state. Ask participants to place a red X next to any of the symptoms they have personally experienced. Ask them to type any additional sensations or ideas into the chat feature. The goal is to identify the physical symptoms of fear. Read additional ideas as they come in through the chat. Ask for participants to elaborate as needed. (Slide 2 of 8)
10:10 a.m. (5 min)	Slide 15 Emotional and Rational Brain • Emotional • Rational Time and perspective help move you from the emotional to the rational brain.	**The Emotional and Rational Brain** • **Handout 8. Emotions and the Brain** Explain the roles of the emotional and rational brain. To make good decisions we need our whole brain to work effectively, yet our emotional brain receives the information first. If we overreact to input, we may find it difficult to handle a situation effectively. Direct participants to record their notes and insights in Part 1 of Handout 8. (Slide 3 of 8)
10:15 a.m. (10 min)	Slide 16 10-Minute Break	**BREAK** Encourage participants to get up and move around. Emphasize that they should try to look away from their computers or phones during the break if possible.

TIMING	SLIDES	ACTIVITIES/NOTES/CONSIDERATIONS
10:25 a.m. (5 min)	Slide 17 Avoid Using Your Reptilian Brain When overcome with emotion, we have a tendency to revert to our untrained nature.	**Emotional Hijacking and the Reptilian Brain** Present the concept of emotional hijacking and the role of our reptilian brain (which is somewhat animalistic and unedited). When we are overcome with emotion, it's as if our brain is "hijacked" and cannot think clearly. You can learn more about emotional hijacking online by searching for the term amygdala hijack. (Slide 4 of 8)
10:30 a.m. (15 min)	Slide 18 Strategies for Gaining Emotional Control • Emotional • Rational Time and perspective help move you from the emotional to the rational brain.	**Strategies for Gaining Emotional Control** • **Handout 8. Emotions and the Brain** Present the idea of an emotional response versus a rational response. Ask participants if they have ever reacted in an emotional way, even if they were trying to remain calm and in control. Use a green check for yes and a red X for no. (Slide 5 of 8)
	Slide 19 Whiteboard What are your best strategies for gaining control when emotions run high?	**Whiteboard Activity** • **Handout 8. Emotions and the Brain** Ask for volunteers to share using the raise hands feature or have participants type their thoughts in the chat feature. Call on individuals to elaborate. Capture ideas on the whiteboard. Direct participants to record their notes and insights in Part 2 of Handout 8. (Slide 6 of 8)
10:45 a.m. (10 min)	Slide 20 Indicators of Relaxation Acetylcholine Calm, Peaceful, Focused	**Indicators of Relaxation** Facilitate a short discussion about the physical indicators of relaxation as a contrast to the earlier discussion of the physical symptoms of fear. Ask participants to place a green check next to any indicators they have experienced personally. Explain that peace and calm trigger the opposite reaction of fear or anger. When your body is relaxed, acetylcholine is produced, which decreases your heart rate, blood pressure, anxiety, and breathing rate. Being calm ultimately enables your brain to stay focused and think clearly. (Slide 7 of 8)

TIMING	SLIDES	ACTIVITIES/NOTES/CONSIDERATIONS
10:55 a.m. (5 min)	Slide 21 Managing the Emotion • Slow down • Focus your thoughts • Breathe deeply • Keep your perspective	**Managing the Emotion** Share these four techniques for managing the impact of emotions on communication. Explain that implementing techniques such as breathing deeply can help buy some time to reframe your perspective and respond to the situation more effectively. Ask participants if they have any other techniques for effectively managing emotions. Have them enter their thoughts in chat and then comment appropriately as they come in. You may want to call on a few people to elaborate. (Slide 8 of 8)
11:00 a.m. (10 min)	Slide 22 Communication Awareness Model Identify emotional trigger Analyze what it makes me think Process how it makes me feel Think about what it makes me want to do Inquire about their side of the story	**Communication Awareness Model** Review the communication awareness model to present the five steps to better communication. It is helpful if you can share a real story to demonstrate the model. Before moving on, ask participants if they have any questions about the model. Use the raise hand function to select speakers.
11:10 a.m. (10 min)	Slide 23 10-Minute Break	**BREAK** Encourage participants to get up and move around. Emphasize that they should try to look away from their computers or phones during the break if possible.

TIMING	SLIDES	ACTIVITIES/NOTES/CONSIDERATIONS
11:20 a.m. (35 min)	Slide 24 Surgical Analysis	**Learning Activity 5. Surgical Analysis of Your Story** • Handout 9. Surgical Analysis of Your Story • Breakout Room Ask participants to reflect on a difficult situation they've experienced recently. Then use the five-step communication awareness model to analyze a challenging conversation. Once they have completed the worksheet, ask them to return to their breakout groups to discuss what they learned about the effectiveness of approaching difficult conversations this way. NOTE: You will want to drop into the breakout rooms to get a sense of what people are discussing so you can better tailor the debrief.
11:55 a.m. (15 min)	Slide 25 Five Steps to Effective Communication Identify emotional trigger Analyze what it makes me think Process how it makes me feel Think about what it makes me want to do Inquire about their side of the story	**Five Steps to Effective Communication** Once the participants have met with their breakout groups, bring them back together to facilitate the group discussion. Use the green check, red X, and raise hand functions to solicit interactions.
12:10 p.m. (10 min)	Slide 26 Morning Process Check	**Morning Debrief** As a morning process check, conduct a large-group discussion about emotion, communication, and having difficult conversations. Use the green check, red X, and raise hand functions to solicit interactions.
12:20 p.m. (60 min)	Slide 27 60-Minute Lunch	**LUNCH** Encourage participants to get up and move around. Emphasize that they should try to look away from their computers or phones during the break if possible. NOTE: If you haven't already done so, create the breakout rooms for pairs to be used in the listening stick exercise.

TIMING	SLIDES	ACTIVITIES/NOTES/CONSIDERATIONS
1:20 p.m. (15 min)	Slide 28 Listening Behavior Assessment	**Assessment 1. Listening Behavior Assessment** Instruct participants to complete the assessment on listening behaviors. The tool also includes instructions to score the assessment. Facilitate a large-group discussion once all participants have completed the instrument. Ask: • What did you notice about yourself? • What were you surprised about? • What should you do differently? Instruct participants to type their responses in chat or on the whiteboard. Read them aloud as they come in, and select one or two people to elaborate. Invite participants to use the raise hand function to add insights or ask questions.
1:35 p.m. (30 min)	Slide 29 Listening Is More Than Hearing	**Learning Activity 6. Listening Is More Than Hearing** • **Handout 28. Speaker's Diagram 1** • **Handout 29. Speaker's Diagram 2** Follow the instructions provided in the learning activity. Debrief the questions using any method you wish (e.g., chat pane or raise hand).
2:05 p.m. (5 min)	Slide 30 Basic Listening Typical, Nonempathetic Listening • Listening: Intending to reply with a solution, opinion, or advice. • Filtering: Screening everything through your own paradigm or agenda. • Evaluating: Determining if you agree or disagree. • Probing: Asking from your frame of reference. • Advising: Giving counsel based on your experience. • Interpreting: Trying to analyze or figure people out.	**Basic Listening** • **Handout 10. Mistakes in Listening** Explain and define the features involved in typical, nonempathetic listening (shown on the slide). The listening skills content starts with "typical" listening and then moves into active listening skills in later slides. Encourage participants to capture notes and insights on the handout.

TIMING	SLIDES	ACTIVITIES/NOTES/CONSIDERATIONS
2:10 p.m. (10 min)	Slide 31 10-Minute Break	**BREAK** Encourage participants to get up and move around. Emphasize that they should try to look away from their computers or phones during the break if possible.
2:20 p.m. (15 min)	Slide 32 Listening Stick (Part 1) Do the following with your partner: 1. Choose an idea you would like to talk about. 2. Each of you will have a chance to talk about the idea for 1 minute. (Pick who goes first.) 3. If you are the talker, simply talk about your idea. 4. If you are the listener, you may not talk. Hold the "stick" as a reminder to listen only!	**Learning Activity 7. Listening Stick (Part 1)** • **Breakout Room** Tell participants that they have been randomly paired and assigned to breakout rooms for this activity. Post the list of pairs on the screen. The objective of this activity is for the participants to experience ineffective listening. Display Slide 32, which provides brief instructions for the participants. Refer to the learning activity for directions on the facilitation process.
2:35 p.m. (15 min)	Slide 33 Principles of Active Listening *Empathetic listening is key to successful relationships. When you sincerely strive to understand people, you try to view the world as they do. You don't have to agree with them, but rather emotionally and intellectually understand them. It involves the ears, eyes, and heart.* Excerpted from Franklin Covey, "Effectiveness Tip of the Week," franklincovey.com.	**Principles of Active Listening (Part 1)** Show the Franklin Covey quote on Slide 29 about active/empathetic listening to introduce the concept of active listening (in contrast to typical listening, which is usually a more common experience). Ask participants to read the quote and give you a green check when they are finished. Wait for green checks. Explain that empathetic/active listening is: • Motivated by a sincere desire to understand • Built one step at a time • Founded on character and trust • Interactive, sincere dialogue • Focused on understanding, not "fixing" (Slide 1 of 4)

TIMING	SLIDES	ACTIVITIES/NOTES/CONSIDERATIONS
	Slide 34	**Principles of Active Listening: Skills**
	Principles of Active Listening • Repeat • Rephrase • Reflect • Rephrase and Reflect	• **Handout 11. Active Listening** Present the four skills at the heart of active, empathetic listening: repeat, rephrase, reflect, rephrase/reflect. Encourage participants to follow along and take notes on the handout. (Slide 2 of 4)
	Slide 35	**Whiteboard Discussion**
	Whiteboard Why rephrase?	Write the question "Why Rephrase?" on the whiteboard. Ask participants to use their text tool to write a brief suggestion on the whiteboard of why it is important to rephrase. Alternately, participants may enter their responses in chat. Select a few to read aloud. Ask if anyone would like to elaborate on their thoughts. Then move to the next slide to explain in more detail why rephrasing is an important aspect of active listening. (Slide 3 of 4)
	Slide 36	**Principles of Active Listening: Rephrasing**
	Why Rephrase? • Clarify understanding • Gain more information • Move toward the answer	• **Handout 11. Active Listening** Explain why rephrasing is important when practicing active listening. (Slide 4 of 4)
2:50 p.m. (15 min)	Slide 37	**Principles of Active Listening: Paraphrasing**
	Examples of Paraphrasing "What I'm hearing you say is _____. Is that right?" "So, in other words, you _____ (think, feel that ...)." "It sounds as if you're saying _____." "Let me make sure I've got this right, you _____."	• **Handout 11. Active Listening** Present tips on rephrasing and paraphrasing. Emphasize the importance of personalizing the approach so you don't sound scripted or insincere. (Slide 1 of 4)

TIMING	SLIDES	ACTIVITIES/NOTES/CONSIDERATIONS
	Slide 38 Whiteboard What is empathy?	**Whiteboard Discussion** Write the question "What is empathy?" on the whiteboard. Ask participants to use their text tool to write a brief phrase on the whiteboard that defines empathy. Alternately, participants may enter their responses in chat. Select a few to read aloud. Ask if anyone would like to elaborate on their thoughts. Then move to the next slide to define and discuss empathy as it relates to active listening. (Slide 2 of 4)
	Slide 39 Empathy Guidelines Empathy expresses how you think the other feels and why. It conveys understanding and builds connection. It does not mean you agree or feel the same way. "It sounds as if you feel _____[feeling], because _____[reason]." "It must be _____[feeling]when _____[reason]." "I can understand that ____[reason]would make you ____[feeling]."	**Principles of Active Listening: Empathy Guidelines** • **Handout 11. Active Listening** Define empathy: "Empathy expresses how you think the other feels and why. It does not mean that you agree or feel the same way." Present guidelines for communicating with empathy. Explain that these sample phrases are meant to be starters to help them practice. It is always better to find your own words so you don't sound scripted or rehearsed. (Slide 3 of 4)
	Slide 40 Listening Stick (Part 2) Do the following with your partner: 1. Decide on an issue that you face in the workplace and would like to discuss. 2. Each person will have a chance to discuss the issue for 5 minutes. (Pick who goes first). 3. Use the listening stick from earlier activity. 4. If you are the talker, explain the scenario and talk. 5. If you are the listener, practice active listening skills (repeat, rephrase, reflect).	**Learning Activity 8. Listening Stick (Part 2)** Display Slide 40 and share this key learning about active listening. (Slide 4 of 4)
3:05 p.m. (10 min)	Slide 41 10-Minute Break	**BREAK** Encourage participants to get up and move around. Emphasize that they should try to look away from their computers or phones during the break if possible.

TIMING	SLIDES	ACTIVITIES/NOTES/CONSIDERATIONS
3:15 p.m. (15 min)	Slide 42 Barriers to Listening What gets in the way of listening?	**Small Group Brainstorm: Barriers to Listening** • **Handout 12. Barriers to Effective Listening** • **Breakout Room** • **Whiteboard** Display the question on Slide 42 and tell participants they will be working in groups to brainstorm things that get in the way of listening. Inform participants that they have been randomly broken into small groups for this learning activity. Show the list of participant assignments on the screen. Ask participants to join their assigned breakout rooms to discuss Handout 12 and record their ideas. Bring everyone back to the main room and ask each group to report what barriers to listening they identified. As participants share, capture their ideas on the whiteboard. Time permitting, you could share a time you experienced a barrier to listening and what happened as a result.
3:30 p.m. (10 min)	Slide 43 Reflection and Action Plan What behaviors will you… •Start? •Stop? •Continue?	**Reflection and Action Plan** • **Handout 13. Reflection and Action Plan** Ask: "What will you do differently as a result of this workshop?" Give participants time to reflect and complete the action plan. This will help them to solidify what they've learned.
3:40 p.m. (10 min)	Slide 44 Summary	**Day 1 Summary: Take Aways** Ask participants to use their text tool to write down the concept that most resonated with them. Alternately, participants may enter their responses in chat. Read the comments aloud and ask for elaboration as needed.

TIMING	SLIDES	ACTIVITIES/NOTES/CONSIDERATIONS
3:50 p.m. (10 min) End 4 p.m.	Slide 45 Q&A	**Close: Final Q&A, Homework, Day 2 Reminders, and Informal Evaluations** Field questions about any Day 1 workshop topics. Assign homework and conduct informal evaluations if applicable. **Homework:** Assign the Personal Case Scenario worksheet (Handout 16) as homework. **Optional:** • **Assessment 2. Communication Style Inventory** The communication style inventory provides a comprehensive assessment of individual communication styles. If you choose to assign this as homework, remember to debrief it on Day 2. • **Learning Activity 24. Informal Evaluations** You may also choose to conduct informal Day 1 evaluations. See Learning Activity 24 for some easy and innovative ideas.

What to Do Between Workshop Days

- Make notes on any questions or follow-up you need to do so you don't forget.

- Capture facilitator lessons learned from the first day of the workshop. Adjust Day 2 materials if needed.

- Deal with any technology or other learning environment issues you weren't able to address during the workshop.

- Get a good night's sleep so you can log in early, refreshed, and ready to go for Day 2.

Two-Day Workshop Agenda: Day 2

Day 2—Facilitator Checklist

✓	TASK	SUGGESTED TIMEFRAME
	Prepare a sample mind map that you can use before slide 50.	Day before the session.
	Log into the workshop a minimum of 30 minutes prior to the start of the session to verify that the content is loaded and working as planned. Make sure to have a printed copy of this guide in front of you.	Day of session.
	Verify the breakout rooms and participant assignments.	Day of session.
	Ensure the desired settings are enabled for the presentation and participants.	Day of session.
	As an audio check and to verify that participants are able to interact as planned, greet each participant verbally as they enter and ask them to write their first name and favorite ice cream flavor (or another random question) on the whiteboard.	Start 15 minutes before the presentation begins. This serves as an initial audio and connectivity check for the annotation and interactivity tools.

Agenda

Day 2 (8 a.m.–4 p.m.)

TIMING	SLIDES	ACTIVITIES/NOTES/CONSIDERATIONS
8 a.m. (10 min)	Slide 46 ATD Workshop Effective Communication Skills Day 2 Reconnect	**Welcome and Reconnect** Briefly welcome back the participants. Ask them to take a few minutes to verify that all their interactivity functions are working as planned. Remind participants that they may be asked to share their screens or cameras as part of the workshop's exercises and activities. Remind participants to complete their personal case scenarios (Handout 16) if they haven't already done so.

TIMING	SLIDES	ACTIVITIES/NOTES/CONSIDERATIONS
8:10 a.m. (15 min)	Slide 47 Revisit Ground Rules and Expectations • Participate! • Explore new ideas • Have fun • "Vegas rule" • What else?	**Revisit Ground Rules and Expectations** Reconfirm ground rules and program expectations. Check on progress toward objectives. If you assigned homework, acknowledge that and answer any questions participants had.
8:25 a.m. (50 min)	Slide 48 Alpha Beta Exercise Exercise rules: • Solve a simple, analytical problem. • Communicate in writing only. • No oral communication permitted. • Deliver your messages through chat. • When you believe you have solved the problem, Alpha or Beta will raise a hand and I will check your answer.	**Learning Activity 9. Alpha Beta Exercise** • **Handout 14. Alpha Beta Exercise** This activity seems more complicated than it is, so be sure to use the full facilitation process and follow instructions in the learning activity. It is a silent activity, so once you explain the directions all participant communication will be done in writing. Show Slide 48 and present the rules for this exercise. Encourage participants to reference their handout during the activity. (Slide 1 of 4)
	Slide 49 Alpha Beta Exercise Communication process: • Only written communication allowed • All communication is sent by direct chat to the messenger for distribution. (Do not send to "all participants.") • Improperly addressed mail will be returned or destroyed	**Learning Activity 9. Alpha Beta Exercise** • **Handout 14. Alpha Beta Exercise** Show Slide 49 and present the rules for the communication process that is used in this exercise. It's important that the organizational hierarchy is strictly followed. Encourage participants to reference the handout during the activity. (Slide 2 of 4)
	Slide 50 Alpha Beta Exercise Addressing Your Messages TO: [recipient] (for example, Alpha) FROM: [sender] (for example, Beta) ❌ **Note:** The messenger will check your mail to ensure it is properly addressed. If not addressed correctly, your messages may be returned to you or lost in cyberspace.	**Learning Activity 9. Alpha Beta Exercise** • **Handout 14. Alpha Beta Exercise** Show Slide 50 and present the format the participants will use to send messages in this exercise. Encourage participants to reference the handout during the activity. (Slide 3 of 4)

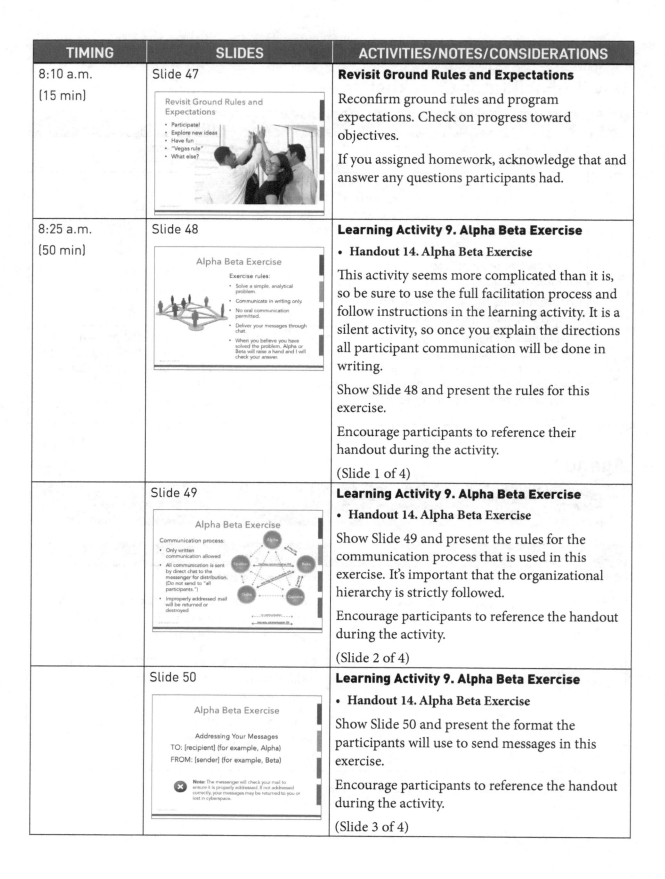

TIMING	SLIDES	ACTIVITIES/NOTES/CONSIDERATIONS
9:15 a.m. (10 min)	Slide 51 Debrief and Discussion How is this experience similar to what really occurs in the workplace?	**Learning Activity 9. Alpha Beta Exercise** • **Handout 14. Alpha Beta Exercise** This activity has the potential to drive a very rich discussion. Debrief the questions using any method you wish (e.g., chat pane or raise hand). Encourage participants to record their insights on the handout. (Slide 4 of 4)
9:25 a.m. (10 min)	Slide 52 10-Minute Break	**BREAK** Encourage participants to get up and move around. Emphasize that they should try to look away from their computers or phones during the break if possible.
9:35 a.m. (5 min)	Slide 53 Whiteboard What makes "good" business writing?	**Discussion** Write: "What makes good business writing?" on the whiteboard. Ask participants to either raise their hand or reply in chat. Capture their ideas on the whiteboard.
9:40 a.m. (10 min)	Slide 54 Model for Effective Business Writing	**Model for Effective Business Writing** • **Handout 15. Model for Effective Business Writing** Introduce the model for effective business writing and summarize the steps. Encourage participants to follow along on Slide 47 or Handout 15.

TIMING	SLIDES	ACTIVITIES/NOTES/CONSIDERATIONS
9:50 a.m. (15 min)	Slide 55 **Planning Your Writing Content** Brainstorming Questions • What is the purpose? • Who is your audience? • What are their needs? • What are your expectations (and theirs)? • What is the core content for your message?	**Planning Your Writing Content** Review the brainstorming questions on Slide 49, and explain how they can be used in the mind-mapping technique.
10:05 a.m. (5 min)	Slide 56 Whiteboard Mind Mapping	Demonstrate the development of a mind map. Each main limb of the map is used for building on the original concept and branching out by adding relevant ideas to the main concept: • Choose a topic to place in the center of the map (for example, an upcoming event). • Label the first limb "audience" and then add additional branches for each stakeholder member identified. • Label the next limb "need" and add branches with answers in that category. • Label another "expectations" and add branches. • Label another "content" and add branches.
10:10 a.m. (15 min)	Slide 57 Document Planning Mind Map Planning to write: • Purpose? • Audience? • Needs? • Expectations? • Core message?	**Learning Activity 11. Document Planning Mind Map** • **Handout 17. Mind Map: Plan Your Content** Now it is your participants' turn. Instruct them to choose a personal case scenario from Handout 16 and map all content planning considerations. Ask participants to give you a green check when they have completed their maps. Debrief the questions using any method you wish (e.g., chat pane or raise hand).
10:25 a.m. (10 min)	Slide 58 10-Minute Break	**BREAK** Encourage participants to get up and move around. Emphasize that they should try to look away from their computers or phones during the break if possible.

TIMING	SLIDES	ACTIVITIES/NOTES/CONSIDERATIONS
10:35 a.m. (10 min)	Slide 59 Brainstorm… Brainstorming!	**Brainstorm . . . Brainstorming!** • Handout 18. Brainstorm Other Brainstorming Methods • Breakout Room Ask participants to join their assigned breakout rooms to brainstorm other brainstorming techniques besides mind mapping. Instruct them to record their insights on the handouts, which also include best practices for productive brainstorming. Bring everyone back to the main room and debrief using any method you wish (e.g., chat pane or raise hand). Capture the responses on the whiteboard.

10:45 a.m.
(5 min)
	Slide 60
	
	Five Cs of Effective Communication
	
	• Clear
	 • Concise
	  • Complete
	   • Correct
	    • Considerate
		Five Cs of Effective Communication
		
		• Handout 19. Five Cs of Effective Communication
		
		Present the Five Cs of Effective Communication. Participants can follow along and take additional notes on the handout.

10:50 a.m. (15 min)	Slide 61 Whiteboard Which of the Five Cs is omitted and why?	**Learning Activity 12. Five Cs** • Whiteboard • Handout 19. Five Cs of Effective Communication • Breakout Room Follow the facilitation instructions in Learning Activity 12. Inform participants that they have been randomly broken into four groups—winter, spring, summer, and fall—for this activity. Display the list of groups on the screen. Ask participants to work in their assigned breakout rooms to identify communication pitfalls. Bring everyone back to the main room and debrief using any method you wish (e.g., chat pane and raise hand). Capture all responses on the whiteboard.

TIMING	SLIDES	ACTIVITIES/NOTES/CONSIDERATIONS

11:05 a.m.
(25 min)
	Slide 62
	
	Practical Practice (Clear)
	
	• Clear
	 • Concise
	  • Complete
	   • Correct
	    • Considerate
		Learning Activity 13. Clear Communication
		• **Handout 20. Practical Practice—Clear Communication**
		• **Breakout Room**
		This exercise gives participants practice writing with clarity by assigning an unexpected task: writing instructions for a Martian!
		Direct them to work as pairs in their breakout rooms so they can check each other's work. Post the list of pair assignments on the screen.
		Follow full facilitation instructions in the learning activity.
		After 15 minutes, bring everyone back to the main room and ask for volunteers to share their instructions with the class.
		Debrief using any method you wish (e.g., chat pane or raise hand).

11:30 a.m.
(15 min)
	Slide 63
	
	Practical Practice (Concise)
	
	• Clear
	 • Concise
	  • Complete
	   • Correct
	    • Considerate
		Learning Activity 14. Concise Communication
		• **Handout 21. Practical Practice—Concise Communication**
		• **Breakout Room**
		This exercise will give participants practice rewriting wordy phrases so only relevant information is included and there's no unnecessary repetition.
		Direct participants back to their paired breakout rooms so they can check each other's work. Follow the full facilitation instructions in the learning activity.
		After 7–8 minutes, bring everyone back to the main room and ask for volunteers to share their responses with the class.
		Debrief using any method you wish (e.g., chat pane or raise hand).

TIMING	SLIDES	ACTIVITIES/NOTES/CONSIDERATIONS

11:45 a.m.
(15 min)
	Slide 64
	
	Practical Practice (Complete)
	
	• Clear
	  • Concise
	    • **Complete**
	      • Correct
	        • Considerate
		Learning Activity 15. Complete Communication
		• **Handout 22. Practical Practice—Complete Communication**
		• **Breakout Room**
		
		This exercise will give participants practice rewriting a business document so that it provides complete information.
		
		Direct participants back to their paired breakout rooms so they can check each other's work. Follow the full facilitation instructions in the learning activity.
		
		After 7–8 minutes, bring everyone back to the main room and ask for volunteers to share their responses with the class.
		
		Debrief using any method you wish (e.g., chat pane or raise hand).

12 p.m. (60 min)	Slide 65 60-Minute Lunch	**LUNCH** Encourage participants to get up and move around. Emphasize that they should try to look away from their computers or phones during the break if possible.

TIMING	SLIDES	ACTIVITIES/NOTES/CONSIDERATIONS
1 p.m. (20 min)	Slide 66 Practical Practice (Correct) • Clear • Concise • Complete • Correct • Considerate	**Learning Activity 16. Correct Communication** • **Handout 23. Practical Practice—Checklist for Correct Communication** • **Breakout Room** This handout provides a list of ideas that are often forgotten when drafting a message. Use it when drafting a business document to make sure it provides the correct information. Direct participants back to their paired breakout rooms to review the checklist and contribute any additional, relevant ideas. Follow the full facilitation instructions in the learning activity. After 7–8 minutes, bring everyone back to the main room and ask for volunteers to share their responses with the class. Debrief using any method you wish (e.g., chat pane or raise hand).
1:20 p.m. (20 min)	Slide 67 Practical Practice (Considerate) • Clear • Concise • Complete • Correct • Considerate	**Learning Activity 17. Considerate Communication: Circles of Influence** • **Handout 24. Practical Practice—Your Role in Considerate Communication** This activity helps participants explore the influences that have shaped them into the people they are today and identify cultural biases and filters that affect considerate communication. Emphasize that each person has a role to play in considerate communication. Follow the facilitation instructions in Learning Activity 17. Use the whiteboard to model the activity for the participants.
1:40 p.m. (15 min)	Slide 68 15-Minute Break	**BREAK** Encourage participants to get up and move around. Emphasize that they should try to look away from their computers or phones during the break if possible.

TIMING	SLIDES	ACTIVITIES/NOTES/CONSIDERATIONS
1:55 p.m. (20 min)	Slide 69 Identifying Your Reader's Needs What is your intent versus what they need to hear? | Needs	Wants | 	**Learning Activity 18. Identify Your Reader's Needs** • **Handout 25. The Wants and Needs of Your Reader** • **Breakout Room** Use your method of choice to facilitate a discussion around the reader's wants and needs. Have participants begin by considering what they themselves want and need as readers and then extrapolate to their audience. This conversation is very helpful for encouraging them to carefully consider and plan the content of their written messages. Your audience is looking to answer these questions: • What is this about, and does it matter to me? • What do I have to do now, and when is it due? • What data do I need to know from this? • How does this make me feel? • Can I skip this all together? Use the breakout rooms to allow groups to complete the worksheet in the handout. After 7–8 minutes, bring everyone back and ask for volunteers to share their responses. Capture their answers in appropriate column on the screen. Debrief the questions using any method you wish (e.g., chat pane or raise hand).

TIMING	SLIDES	ACTIVITIES/NOTES/CONSIDERATIONS
2:15 p.m. (30 min)	Slide 70 Draft Your Message Draft the Message Five Cs	Clear	Concise	Complete	Considerate	Correct	**Learning Activity 19. Draft Your Message** • **Handout 26. Draft Your Message** • **Breakout Room** This activity helps participants practice drafting a document that considers the needs of the reader and conforms to the Five Cs (clear, concise, complete, correct, and considerate). Direct participants back to their paired breakout rooms to share their thoughts and provide each other feedback. Show the list of assignments on the screen. Follow the full facilitation instructions in Learning Activity 19. After 15 minutes, bring everyone back and ask for volunteers to share their responses with the class. Debrief using any method you wish (e.g., chat pane or raise hand).
2:45 p.m. (10 min)	Slide 71 Debrief and Discussion How is this experience similar to what really occurs in the workplace?	**Most Commonly Forgotten Communication Factors** It is helpful to discuss the Five Cs from a big-picture perspective. Use Slide 71 as a focal point for a final wrap-up conversation before participants take the last step of designing the document. Encourage input using any method you wish (e.g., chat pane or raise hand).
2:55 p.m. (10 min)	Slide 72 10-Minute Break	**BREAK** Encourage participants to get up and move around. Emphasize that they should try to look away from their computers or phones during the break if possible.

TIMING	SLIDES	ACTIVITIES/NOTES/CONSIDERATIONS
3:05 p.m. (10 minutes)	Slide 73 Design the Document	**Design the Document** Once crafted, great communication goes an extra step and incorporates design—not only what it says, but what it looks like. Review design considerations with participants, including whitespace, paragraph length, fonts, and bullet points.
3:15 p.m. (15 minutes)	Slide 74 Reflection and Action Plan What behaviors will you… • Start? • Stop? • Continue?	**Reflection and Action Plan** • **Handout 27. Reflection and Action Plan** Ask: "What will you do differently as a result of this class?" Solicit input using any method you wish (e.g., chat pane or raise hand). Capture any comments on the whiteboard. Allow participants time to reflect and complete the action plan. This will help them solidify what they've learned.
3:30 p.m. (15 minutes)	Slide 75 Summary	**Discussion: Day 2 Summary** Facilitate a discussion and solicit feedback about the best take-aways from the course. Capture their responses on the whiteboard.
3:45 p.m. (15 minutes) End 4 p.m.	Slide 76 Q&A	**Close: Final Q&A and Evaluation** • **Assessment 3. Course Evaluation** Field questions about any Day 2 topics or the workshop as a whole. Share any final details or follow-up activities (see chapter 9 for ideas for follow-up coaching). Distribute the session evaluations (Assessment 3). Consider including an inspiring quote or story to close the workshop on a positive note.

What to Do Next

- Determine the training schedule; confirm which platform you're using and familiarize yourself with it.

- Identify and invite participants.

- Inform participants about and distribute any prework. Consider using self-assessment instruments (such as Assessment 1. Listening Behavior Assessment or Assessment 2. Communication Style Inventory).

- Review the workshop objectives, activities, and handouts to plan the content you will use.

- Prepare the participant materials and any activity-related extras for electronic distribution. Refer to chapter 13 for information on how to access and use the included supplemental materials.

- Prepare yourself both emotionally and physically. Make sure you have taken care of any scheduling conflicts or personal challenges (as best you can), so you can be fully present to facilitate the class.

- Get a good night's sleep before you facilitate the workshop so you have the energy and focus to deliver a great class!

Reference

Mehrabian, A. (1981). *Silent Messages: Implicit Communication of Emotions and Attitudes*, 2nd ed. Belmont, CA: Wadsworth.

Chapter 2
One-Day Communication Skills Workshop

What's in This Chapter

- Objectives of the one-day communication skills workshop
- Summary chart for the flow of content and activities
- One-day program agenda

There are a couple of different approaches to holding a one-day workshop. You can choose a theme and provide a deep dive into one aspect of communication, or you can take a broader look at a variety of topics such as listening, oral communication, virtual communication, challenging discussions, or written communication. The challenge of the latter approach of including a number of different aspects of communication in a one-day workshop is that there is very little time to explore the topics in depth or to practice the skills; at the end of the day the participant may leave the workshop with a lot of information and very little practiced skill.

For that reason, this one-day workshop is deliberately designed with the deep-dive approach in mind. In one day, participants can explore a concentrated topic more thoroughly, as well as have the opportunity to practice the skills they are learning. There is also more time for discussion and reflection to enhance learning and retention. As with the two-day workshop design, an effective one-day workshop must account for and anticipate the natural and predictable low energy times during the day. Activities that engage participants in relevant and meaningful small-group discussion and practice are essential to a successful training event.

A full-day workshop requires the facilitator to have a high level of energy and focus and a keen ability to read the energy level of the participants throughout the duration of the program. You can keep your participants engaged and the energy high by managing the flow of activities, presentations, and small- or large-group discussions. Consider changing your training method every 10 to 15 minutes.

This chapter provides a one-day workshop agenda using active training techniques. It is designed to keep the content relevant, meaningful, and interactive. The day begins with one of the most important aspects of communication: listening. Throughout the day, the content focuses on how to listen actively and how to deliver your message effectively.

One-Day Workshop Objectives

By the end of the one-day workshop, participants will be able to:

- Assess their personal listening skills
- Explain and practice active listening skills
- Determine the best way to get their points across
- Identify the most common barriers to communication
- Explore the role emotion plays in communication and discuss strategies and techniques for managing its impact

One-Day Workshop Overview

Workshop Overview

TOPICS	TIMING
Welcome and Introduction	10 minutes
Learning Activity 1. Objective Decision	15 minutes
Ground Rules and Expectations	10 minutes
Learning Activity 2. The Most Difficult Person	15 minutes
Assessment 1. Listening Behavior Assessment	15 minutes
BREAK	**10 minutes**
Learning Activity 6. Listening Is More Than Hearing	30 minutes
Basic Listening	10 minutes
Learning Activity 7. The Listening Stick (Part 1)	15 minutes
BREAK	**10 minutes**
Principles of Active Listening (Part 1) Skills and Rephrasing	15 minutes
Principles of Active Listening (Part 2) Paraphrasing and Empathy	15 minutes

TOPICS	TIMING
Learning Activity 8. Listening Stick (Part 2)	20 minutes
Small Group Brainstorm: Barriers to Listening	15 minutes
Morning Debrief	10 minutes
LUNCH	**60 minutes**
Communication Model Process	10 minutes
Learning Activity 3. Identify the Noise	15 minutes
The Communication Pie (Three Modes of Communication)	10 minutes
Learning Activity 4. Impression Improv	20 minutes
Congruent Communication	5 minutes
Incongruent Communication	5 minutes
BREAK	**10 minutes**
Vocal Tone and Word Emphasis	10 minutes
The Role of Emotion in Communication	5 minutes
The Emotional and Rational Brain	5 minutes
Emotional Hijacking and the Reptilian Brain	5 minutes
Strategies for Gaining Emotional Control	15 minutes
Managing the Emotion	5 minutes
Communication Awareness Model	10 minutes
BREAK	**10 minutes**
Learning Activity 5. Surgical Analysis of Your Story	35 minutes
Reflection and Action Plan	10 minutes
Summary: Take Aways	10 minutes
Final Q&A and Evaluations	10 minutes
TOTAL	**480 minutes (8 hours)**

Considerations for the Virtual Environment

Conducting a workshop in a virtual format is often necessary to provide benefits of time and location flexibility as well as to account for cost. Unfortunately, this modality also brings the risk of some challenges, such as technology limitations, distracted learners, a lack of nonverbal cues, and the highly beneficial informal, but relevant, sidebar conversations that take place among learners in a shared space with a shared interest. When considering conducting a workshop in a virtual format, the following recommendations may help minimize some of these risks:

- Consider breaking up the content into smaller chunks. Ideally, virtual sessions should be no longer than two to four hours a day. See chapter 4 for suggestions on how this content can be grouped into shorter or topic-specific sessions.

- To keep participants engaged, ensure that you maintain a high level of energy and frequently solicit input, both verbal and through the use of the technology tools throughout the duration of the workshop.
- Actively seek frequent feedback from participants to gauge their understanding.
- Use the video feature as much as possible so that participants can see that they have an instructor who is working with them and not just sharing static slides on a screen.
- Encourage participants to use their video features when speaking to help better engage with one another.

Preparation

While all facilitation sessions require preparation, the success of a virtual session is even more dependent on how carefully the facilitator prepares and the completion of a thorough and deliberate setup. The following checklists have been provided to help you ensure a smooth and effective workshop delivery. Please note, these checklists have been created with a WebEx environment in mind. As technologies and platforms can differ, you are encouraged to modify these recommendations based on the specific needs of your delivery.

Pre-Workshop—Facilitator Checklist

✓	TASK	SUGGESTED TIMEFRAME
	Upload the presentation files.	One week prior to the session.
	Review the facilitator guide and any other course materials.	Ideally, one week prior to the start of the session, but no later than 72 hours in advance.
	Validate the final participant list.	Ideally, one week prior to the start of the session, but no later than 72 hours in advance.
	Send a welcome email to participants. Let them know you are looking forward to the class, and include reminders to complete any necessary prework and to verify connection and compatibility. Highlight the fact that this is designed to be an interactive workshop, which means that they may be asked to share their screen and video camera during the sessions so may want to ensure appropriate and respectful appearance and attire. In addition, they will be asked to interact with others in the session frequently and will need to minimize any external distractions to get the most favorable learning experience from the course.	One week prior to the session.

✓	TASK	SUGGESTED TIMEFRAME
	Create polls and breakout rooms.	At least 72 hours before the session.
	Ensure you're familiar with how the interactivity functionality within your presentation platform works. You need to be able to explain this to participants. You may also want to create a short cheat sheet that you can use to demonstrate these functions as you welcome participants to the session. This is particularly important if you are conducting a session for participants from multiple organizations.	At least 72 hours before the session.

Create Polls

Create these polls before the start of the workshop. Ensure that each poll is set to share responses with all participants.

✓	LOCATION	POLL RESPONSES
	Slide 2 (Objectives)	• Assess your personal listening skills. • Explain and practice active listening skills. • Determine the best way to get your point across. • Identify the most common barriers of communication. • Explore the role emotion plays in communication and discuss strategies and techniques for managing its impact.
	Slide 77	• Speaker • Listener
	Slide 8	• Words we use • How we say words, tone of voice, style • Facial expression, body language

Create Breakout Rooms

Create these breakout rooms before the start of the workshop. Create a list of who has been assigned to each room that you can display onscreen at the start of the activity.

✓	ROOM DESCRIPTION	NOTES
	Create enough breakout rooms that the participants can be split into groups of five or fewer. Randomly assign each participant to a room so that the groups are roughly equal in number. Label rooms: • Room 1 • Room 2 • Room 3 • Room 4 • and so on	You will use these breakout rooms for the following activities: • Barriers to Listening • Learning Activity 3. Identify the Noise • Learning Activity 5. Surgical Analysis of Your Story
	Create enough breakout rooms to accommodate breaking the group up into pairs. For example, if you have 20 participants, you will need 10 breakout rooms. Randomly assign each participant to a room. Label rooms: • Pair 1 • Pair 2 • Pair 3 • Pair 4 • and so on	You will use these breakout rooms for the following activity: • Learning Activity 7. Listening Stick (Part 1) • Learning Activity 8. Listening Stick (Part 2)

One-Day Workshop Agenda

Day 1 (8 a.m. to 4 p.m.)

TIMING	SLIDES	ACTIVITIES/NOTES/CONSIDERATIONS
8 a.m. (10 min)	Slide 1 ATD Workshop Effective Communication Skills	**Welcome and Introduction** Briefly welcome the participants and introduce yourself. Provide a quick overview of the functionality and interactivity elements that will be used during the session (e.g., polls, chat, whiteboard, breakout sessions). A sample functionality overview has been provided. This sample is specific to the WebEx environment. Ensure that participants are aware that they may be asked to share their screens or cameras as part of the exercises and activities during the workshop.
8:10 a.m. (15 min)	Slide 2 Two-Day Workshop Objectives • Identify the most common barriers of communication. • Explain the Five Cs of Effective Communication. • Assess your listening skills. • Explain and practice active listening skills. • Determine the best way to get your point across. • Examine situational dynamics to assess the best approach for communicating in challenging situations. • Apply effective principles for face-to-face, written, and virtual scenarios.	**Learning Activity 1. Objective Decision** • **Handout 1b. Objective Decision** • **Poll: Objectives** This activity provides an innovative way to facilitate the discussion about session objectives rather than simply reading them to the participants. Ask participants to follow the instructions in the handout. When they are finished ask them to use the poll to select the objective that corresponds to the one they highlighted. Share poll results with all.

TIMING	SLIDES	ACTIVITIES/NOTES/CONSIDERATIONS
8:25 a.m. (10 min)	Slide 3 Ground Rules and Expectations • Participate! • Explore new ideas • Have fun. • "Vegas rule" • What else?	**Ground Rules and Expectations** Facilitate a discussion about ground rules and expectations for the course. Adjust times as needed for starting, breaks, and lunches. It is important to establish a positive learning environment. Ask participants to give you a green check if they are in agreement with the ground rules for the session.
8:35 a.m. (15 min)	Slide 4 Whiteboard Who is the most difficult person in the world?	**Learning Activity 2. The Most Difficult Person** • **Handout 2. The Most Difficult Person in the World** Get participants thinking by using Handout 2. Debrief the questions using any method you wish (e.g., chat pane or raise hand). Capture responses on the whiteboard so that all can see.
8:50 a.m. (15 min)	Slide 28 Listening Behavior Assessment	**Assessment 1. Listening Behavior Assessment** Instruct participants to complete the assessment on listening behaviors. The tool also includes instructions to score the assessment. Facilitate a large-group discussion once all participants have completed the instrument. Ask: • What did you notice about yourself? • What were you surprised about? • What should you do differently? Instruct participants to type their responses in chat or on the whiteboard. Read them aloud as they come in, and select one or two people to elaborate. Invite participants to use the raise hand function to add insights or ask questions.

TIMING	SLIDES	ACTIVITIES/NOTES/CONSIDERATIONS
9:05 a.m. (10 min)	Slide 16 10-Minute Break	**BREAK** Encourage participants to get up and move around. Emphasize that they should try to look away from their computers or phones during the break if possible.
9:15 a.m. (30 min)	Slide 29 Listening Is More Than Hearing	**Learning Activity 6. Listening Is More Than Hearing** Follow the instructions provided in the learning activity. Debrief the questions using any method you wish (e.g., chat pane or raise hand).
9:45 a.m. (10 min)	Slide 30 Basic Listening Typical, Nonempathetic Listening • Listening: Intending to reply with a solution, opinion, or advice. • Filtering: Screening everything through your own paradigm or agenda. • Evaluating: Determining if you agree or disagree. • Probing: Asking from your frame of reference. • Advising: Giving counsel based on your experience. • Interpreting: Trying to analyze or figure people out.	**Basic Listening** • **Handout 10. Mistakes in Listening** Explain and define the features involved in typical, nonempathetic listening (shown on the slide). The listening skills content starts with "typical" listening and then moves into active listening skills in later slides. Encourage participants to capture notes and insights on the handout.
9:55 a.m. (15 min)	Slide 32 Listening Stick (Part 1) Do the following with your partner: 1. Choose an idea you would like to talk about. 2. Each of you will have a chance to talk about the idea for 1 minute. (Pick who goes first.) 3. If you are the talker, simply talk about your idea. 4. If you are the listener, you may not talk. Hold the "stick" as a reminder to listen only!	**Learning Activity 7. Listening Stick (Part 1)** • **Breakout Room** Tell participants that they have been randomly paired and assigned to breakout rooms for this activity. Post the list of pairs on the screen. The objective of this activity is for the participants to experience ineffective listening. Display Slide 32, which provides brief instructions for the participants. Refer to the learning activity for directions on the facilitation process.

TIMING	SLIDES	ACTIVITIES/NOTES/CONSIDERATIONS
10:10 a.m. (10 min)	Slide 16 10-Minute Break	**BREAK** Encourage participants to get up and move around. Emphasize that they should try to look away from their computers or phones during the break if possible.
10:20 a.m. (15 min)	Slide 33 Principles of Active Listening *Empathetic listening is key to successful relationships. When you sincerely strive to understand people, you try to view the world as they do. You don't have to agree with them, but rather emotionally and intellectually understand them. It involves the ears, eyes, and heart.* Excerpted from Franklin Covey, "Effectiveness Tip of the Week," franklincovey.com.	**Principles of Active Listening (Part 1)** Show the Franklin Covey quote on Slide 30 about active/empathetic listening to introduce the concept of active listening (in contrast to typical listening, which is usually a more common experience). Ask participants to read the quote and give you a green check when they are finished. Wait for green checks. Explain that empathetic/active listening is: • Motivated by a sincere desire to understand • Built one step at a time • Founded on character and trust • Interactive, sincere dialogue • Focused on understanding, not "fixing" (Slide 1 of 4)
	Slide 34 Principles of Active Listening • Repeat • Rephrase • Reflect • Rephrase and Reflect	**Principles of Active Listening (Part 1): Skills** • **Handout 11. Active Listening** Present the four skills at the heart of active, empathetic listening: repeat, rephrase, reflect, rephrase/reflect. Encourage participants to follow along and take notes on the handout. (Slide 2 of 4)

TIMING	SLIDES	ACTIVITIES/NOTES/CONSIDERATIONS
	Slide 35 Whiteboard Why rephrase?	Write the question "Why Rephrase?" on the whiteboard. Ask participants to use their text tool to write a brief note on the whiteboard that suggests why it is important to rephrase. Alternately, participants may enter their responses in chat. Select a few to read aloud. Ask if anyone would like to elaborate on their thoughts. Then move to the next slide to explain in more detail why rephrasing is an important aspect of active listening. (Slide 3 of 4)
	Slide 36 Why Rephrase? • Clarify understanding • Gain more information • Move toward the answer	**Principles of Active Listening (Part 1): Rephrasing** • **Handout 11. Active Listening** Explain why rephrasing is important when practicing active listening. (Slide 4 of 4)
10:35 a.m. (15 min)	Slide 37 Examples of Paraphrasing "What I'm hearing you say is _____. Is that right?" "So, in other words, you _____ (think, feel that …)." "It sounds as if you're saying _____." "Let me make sure I've got this right, you _____."	**Principles of Active Listening (Part 2): Paraphrasing** • **Handout 11. Active Listening** Present tips on rephrasing and paraphrasing. Emphasize the importance of personalizing the approach so you don't sound scripted or insincere. (Slide 1 of 3)
	Slide 38 Whiteboard What is empathy?	Write the question "What is empathy?" on the whiteboard. Ask participants to use their text tool to write a brief phrase on the whiteboard that defines empathy. Alternately, participants may enter their responses in chat. Select a few to read aloud. Ask if anyone would like to elaborate on their thoughts. Then move to the next slide to define and discuss empathy as it relates to active listening. (Slide 2 of 3)

TIMING	SLIDES	ACTIVITIES/NOTES/CONSIDERATIONS
	Slide 39	**Principles of Active Listening (Part 2): Empathy Guidelines**
	Empathy Guidelines	• **Handout 11. Active Listening**
	Empathy expresses how you think the other feels and why. It conveys understanding and builds connection. It does not mean you agree or feel the same way.	Define empathy: "Empathy expresses how you think the other feels and why. It does not mean that you agree or feel the same way."
	"It sounds as if you feel _____ [feeling], because _____ [reason]." "It must be _____ [feeling] when _____ [reason]." "I can understand that _____ [reason] would make you _____ [feeling]."	Present guidelines for communicating with empathy. Explain that these sample phrases are meant to be starters to help them practice. It is always better to find your own words so you don't sound scripted or rehearsed.
		(Slide 3 of 3)
10:50 a.m. (20 min)	Slide 40	**Learning Activity 8. Listening Stick (Part 2)**
	Listening Stick (Part 2)	Tell participants that they will return to their pair breakout rooms for this activity. Post the list of pairs on the screen.
	Do the following with your partner: 1. Decide on an issue that you face in the workplace and would like to discuss. 2. Each person will have a chance to discuss the issue for 5 minutes. (Pick who goes first.) 3. Use the listening stick from earlier activity. 4. If you are the talker, explain the scenario and talk. 5. If you are the listener, practice active listening skills (repeat, rephrase, reflect).	The objective of this activity is for participants to experience and practice active listening. Display Slide 40, which provides brief instructions for the participants. Refer to the learning activity for directions on the facilitation process.
		(Slide 1 of 3)
	Slide 77	Conduct a poll asking participants which role they preferred.
	Poll	• Speaker
	Which role did you prefer: • Speaker • Listener	• Listener
		Select a few people at random to elaborate on their experience and response.
		(Slide 2 of 3)
	Slide 78	Display Slide 78 to share this key information about active listening.
	Active Listening	(Slide 3 of 3)
	These skills are only the beginning. Active listening requires actually caring abut the person you are with, as well as a willingness to invest your time and attention.	

TIMING	SLIDES	ACTIVITIES/NOTES/CONSIDERATIONS
11:10 a.m. (15 min)	Slide 42 Barriers to Listening What gets in the way of listening?	**Small Group Brainstorm: Barriers to Listening** • **Handout 12. Barriers to Effective Listening** • **Breakout Room** • **Whiteboard** Display the question on Slide 42 and tell participants they will be working in groups to brainstorm things that get in the way of listening. Inform participants that they have been randomly broken into small groups for this learning activity. Show the list of participant assignments on the screen. Ask participants to join their assigned breakout rooms to discuss Handout 12 and record their ideas. Bring everyone back to the main room and ask each group to report what barriers to listening they identified. As participants share, capture their ideas on the whiteboard. Time permitting, you could share a time you experienced a barrier to listening and what happened as a result.
11:25 a.m. (10 min)	Slide 26 Morning Process Check	**Morning Debrief** As a morning process check, conduct a large-group discussion about emotion, communication, and having difficult conversations. Use the green check, red X, or raise hand functions to solicit interactions.
11:35 a.m. (60 min)	Slide 27 60-Minute Lunch	**LUNCH** Encourage participants to get up and move around. Emphasize that they should try to look away from their computers or phones during the break if possible.

TIMING	SLIDES	ACTIVITIES/NOTES/CONSIDERATIONS
12:35 p.m. (10 min)	Slide 5 Communication Process Me — My Message — Words — My Message — You Interpreter/Decoder Feedback: My clouded perception of your message to me	**Communication Model Process** Present the communication process diagram (Slide 5). Explain the process of miscommunication and how "noise"—real and perceived—can influence the communication process.
12:45 p.m. (15 min)	Slide 7 Identify the Noise EXTERNAL NOISE! INTERNAL NOISE?	**Learning Activity 3. Identify the Noise** • **Handout 3. Causes of Miscommunication** • **Breakout Room** Direct participants to the handout. Tell participants that they will be working in groups to identify and discuss the sources of noise that create miscommunication. Show the list of breakout room assignments on the screen. Give the groups 5–7 minutes to complete the handout. Bring everyone back to the main room and debrief the questions using any method you wish (e.g., chat pane or raise hand). Be sure to capture the ideas on the whiteboard.
	Slide 8 Poll Rank the importance of three aspects of communication: • Words we use • How we say words (tone of voice and style) • Facial expression and body language	**Poll** Ask participants to rank the importance of three aspects of communication: • Words we use • How we say words, tone of voice, style • Facial expression and body language Share the poll results and introduce the next slide.

TIMING	SLIDES	ACTIVITIES/NOTES/CONSIDERATIONS
1 p.m. (10 min)	Slide 9 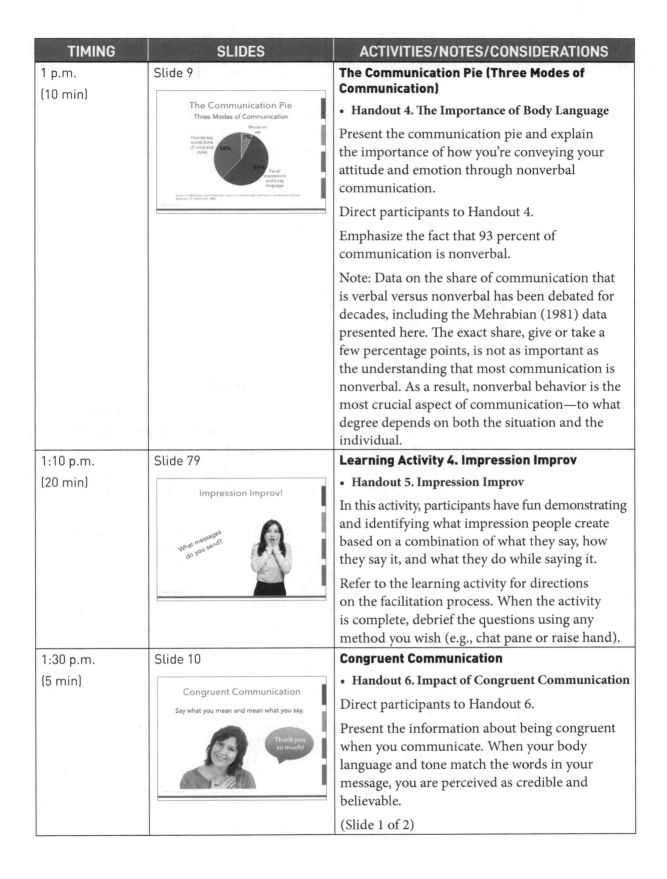	**The Communication Pie (Three Modes of Communication)** • **Handout 4. The Importance of Body Language** Present the communication pie and explain the importance of how you're conveying your attitude and emotion through nonverbal communication. Direct participants to Handout 4. Emphasize the fact that 93 percent of communication is nonverbal. Note: Data on the share of communication that is verbal versus nonverbal has been debated for decades, including the Mehrabian (1981) data presented here. The exact share, give or take a few percentage points, is not as important as the understanding that most communication is nonverbal. As a result, nonverbal behavior is the most crucial aspect of communication—to what degree depends on both the situation and the individual.
1:10 p.m. (20 min)	Slide 79	**Learning Activity 4. Impression Improv** • **Handout 5. Impression Improv** In this activity, participants have fun demonstrating and identifying what impression people create based on a combination of what they say, how they say it, and what they do while saying it. Refer to the learning activity for directions on the facilitation process. When the activity is complete, debrief the questions using any method you wish (e.g., chat pane or raise hand).
1:30 p.m. (5 min)	Slide 10	**Congruent Communication** • **Handout 6. Impact of Congruent Communication** Direct participants to Handout 6. Present the information about being congruent when you communicate. When your body language and tone match the words in your message, you are perceived as credible and believable. (Slide 1 of 2)

TIMING	SLIDES	ACTIVITIES/NOTES/CONSIDERATIONS
1:35 p.m. (5 min)	Slide 11 **Incongruent Communication** *When your tone and body language don't match the message, the words lose their meaning, or the message completely changes.* Thank you so much!	**Incongruent Communication** When communication is incongruent, your body language and tone do not match the words in your message, and you will come across as insincere, disingenuous, and possibly manipulative. (Slide 2 of 2)
1:40 p.m. (10 min)	Slide 16 10-Minute Break	**BREAK** Encourage participants to get up and move around. Emphasize that they should try to look away from their computers or phones during the break if possible.
1:50 p.m. (10 min)	Slide 12 I didn't steal your cow yesterday.	**Vocal Tone and Word Emphasis** The key point here is that your words send different messages depending on the tone and emphasis you use. Say, "I didn't steal your cow yesterday," six times. Each time emphasize a different word (*I, didn't, steal, your, cow,* and *yesterday*) and see how the meaning changes. For example, when you emphasize "I," it can sound as if you didn't steal the cow, but you know who did. To create class interaction, ask different participants to say the sentence while emphasizing a different word. Use the raise hand feature to ask for volunteers. This is a great place to point out how being in a virtual setting can influence the way a message is heard by the audience. This is especially true if you're not using a camera because the audience doesn't have the benefit of seeing any nonverbal cues.

TIMING	SLIDES	ACTIVITIES/NOTES/CONSIDERATIONS
2 p.m. (5 min)	Slide 13 The Role of Emotion in Communication	**The Role of Emotion in Communication** • **Handout 7. The Role of Emotion in Communication** This transition slide helps you shift the focus to the relationship between emotion and communication. Briefly discuss how quickly strong emotions can derail communication. Direct participants to Handout 7. Ask participants if they have experienced a situation where emotions derailed communication. Use a green check for yes and red X for no. Ask participants to raise their hand to share their experiences. Perhaps even tell a story about when this happened to you. (Slide 1 of 6)
2:05 p.m. (5 min)	Slide 15 Emotional and Rational Brain • Emotional • Rational *Time and perspective help move you from the emotional to the rational brain.*	**The Emotional and Rational Brain** • **Handout 8. Emotions and the Brain** Explain the roles of the emotional and rational brain. To make good decisions we need our whole brain to work effectively, yet our emotional brain receives the information first. If we overreact to input, we may find it difficult to handle a situation effectively. Direct participants to record their notes and insights in Part 1 of Handout 8. (Slide 2 of 6)
2:10 p.m. (5 min)	Slide 17 Avoid Using Your Reptilian Brain When overcome with emotion, we have a tendency to revert to our untrained nature.	**Emotional Hijacking and the Reptilian Brain** Present the concept of emotional hijacking and the role of our reptilian brain (which is somewhat animalistic and unedited). When we are overcome with emotion, it's as if our brain is "hijacked" and cannot think clearly. You can learn more about emotional hijacking online by searching for the term amygdala hijack. (Slide 3 of 6)

TIMING	SLIDES	ACTIVITIES/NOTES/CONSIDERATIONS
2:15 p.m. (15 min)	Slide 18 Strategies for Gaining Emotional Control • Emotional • Rational *Time and perspective help move you from the emotional to the rational brain.*	**Strategies for Gaining Emotional Control** • **Handout 8. Emotions and the Brain** Present the idea of an emotional response versus a rational response. Ask participants if they have ever reacted in an emotional way, even if they were trying to remain calm and in control. Use a green check for yes and a red X for no. (Slide 4 of 6)
	Slide 19 Whiteboard What are your best strategies for gaining control when emotions run high?	**Whiteboard Discussion** • **Handout 8. Emotions and the Brain** Ask for volunteers to share using the raise hands feature or have participants type their thoughts in the chat feature. Call on individuals to elaborate. Capture ideas on the whiteboard. Direct participants to record their notes and insights in Part 2 of Handout 8. (Slide 5 of 6)
2:30 p.m. (5 min)	Slide 21 Managing the Emotion • Slow down • Focus your thoughts • Breathe deeply • Keep your perspective	**Managing the Emotion** Share these four techniques for managing the impact of emotions on communication. Explain that implementing techniques such as breathing deeply can help buy some time to reframe your perspective and respond to the situation more effectively. Ask participants if they have any other techniques for effectively managing emotions. You may want to call on a few people to elaborate. (Slide 6 of 6)
2:35 p.m. (10 min)	Slide 22 Communication Awareness Model Identify emotional trigger Analyze what it makes me think Process how it makes me feel Think about what it makes me want to do Inquire about their side of the story	**Communication Awareness Model** Review the communication awareness model to present the five steps to better communication. It is helpful if you can share a real story to demonstrate the model. Before moving on, ask participants if they have any questions about the model. Use the raise hand function to select speakers.

TIMING	SLIDES	ACTIVITIES/NOTES/CONSIDERATIONS
2:45 p.m. (10 min)	Slide 23 10-Minute Break	**BREAK** Encourage participants to get up and move around. Emphasize that they should try to look away from their computers or phones during the break if possible.
2:55 p.m. (35 min)	Slide 24 Surgical Analysis	**Learning Activity 5. Surgical Analysis of Your Story** • **Handout 9. Surgical Analysis of Your Story** • **Breakout Room** Ask participants to reflect on a difficult situation they've experienced recently. Then use the five-step communication awareness model to analyze a challenging conversation. Once they have completed the worksheet, ask them to return to their breakout groups to discuss what they learned about the effectiveness of approaching difficult conversations this way. NOTE: You will want to drop into the breakout rooms to get a sense of what people are discussing so that you can better tailor the debrief. Bring everyone back to debrief the questions using any method you wish (e.g., chat pane or raise hand).
3:30 p.m. (10 min)	Slide 43 Reflection and Action Plan What behaviors will you… •Start? •Stop? •Continue?	**Reflection and Action Plan** • **Handout 13. Reflection and Action Plan** Ask: "What will you do differently as a result of this workshop?" Give participants time to reflect and complete the action plan. This will help them to solidify what they've learned.

TIMING	SLIDES	ACTIVITIES/NOTES/CONSIDERATIONS
3:40 p.m. (10 min)	Slide 44 Summary	**Summary: Take Aways** Ask participants to use their text tool to write down the concept that most resonated with them. Alternately, participants may enter their responses in chat. Read the comments aloud and ask for elaboration as needed.
3:50 p.m. (10 min) End 4:00 p.m.	Slide 45 Q&A	**Close: Final Q&A and Evaluations** Field questions about the workshop topics. Share plans for follow-up coaching if applicable (see chapter 10 for ideas for support and activities to follow up). Consider including an inspiring quote or story to close the workshop on a positive note. **Optional:** • **Learning Activity 24. Informal Evaluations** • **Assessment 3. Course Evaluation** You may also conduct informal evaluations (see Learning Activity 24 for easy and innovative ideas) or you can distribute Assessment 3, which is a more formal evaluation participants can complete.

What to Do Next

- Determine the training schedule; confirm which platform you're going to use and familiarize yourself with it.

- Identify and invite participants.

- Inform participants about and distribute any prework. Consider using self-assessment instruments (such as Assessment 1. Listening Behavior Assessment or Assessment 2. Communication Style Inventory).

- Review the workshop objectives, activities, and handouts to plan the content you will use.

- Prepare the participant materials and any activity-related extras for electronic distribution. Refer to chapter 13 for information on how to access and use the included supplemental materials.

- Prepare yourself both emotionally and physically. Make sure you have taken care of any scheduling conflicts or personal challenges (as best you can), so you can be fully present to facilitate the class.

- Get a good night's sleep before you facilitate the workshop so you have the energy and focus to deliver a great class!

Reference

Mehrabian, A. (1981). *Silent Messages: Implicit Communication of Emotions and Attitudes*, 2nd ed. Belmont, CA: Wadsworth.

Chapter 3

Half-Day Communication Skills Workshop

What's in This Chapter

- Objectives of the half-day communication skills workshop
- Summary chart for the flow of content and activities
- Half-day program agenda

When creating a half-day workshop, the time constraints present you with two choices: Choose one communication theme and explore it more thoroughly, or choose a variety of communication topics and cover them in less depth. The challenge with the scattershot approach is that there is very little time to practice the skills; at the end of the day participants may leave the workshop with a lot of information and very little practiced skill.

If you choose a deeper dive into a specific theme, however, participants have the opportunity to practice the skills they are learning. For that reason, the content for the half-day workshop presented in this chapter focuses on organizational communication and the impact of assumptions and poorly communicated messages. If your needs analysis revealed that the learners in a particular organization needed more emphasis on *written* communication, you could instead choose to modify and use the Day 2 agenda from the two-day workshop. In addition, chapter 4 gives many options for customizing the content and activities for specific business needs that would fit easily into a half-day format. (See chapter 5 for more on identifying needs for communication skills training.)

Any workshop, regardless of length, benefits from incorporating the principles of active training. This workshop is designed to present activities that engage participants in relevant and meaningful learning experiences, small group discussion, and skills practice. Be sure to allow time for discussion and reflection to enhance learning and retention.

Half-Day Workshop Objectives

By the end of the half-day workshop, participants will be able to:

- Identify the most common barriers of organizational communication.
- Examine organizational dynamics to assess the best approach for communicating in challenging situations.
- Explain the Five Cs of Effective Communication (clear, concise, complete, correct, and considerate).
- Draft a message that uses all Five Cs.

Half-Day Workshop Overview

TOPICS	TIMING
Welcome and Introduction	10 minutes
Learning Activity 1. Objective Decision	10 minutes
Ground Rules and Expectations	5 minutes
Learning Activity 9. Alpha Beta Exercise	50 minutes
BREAK	**10 minutes**
Activity Debrief: Alpha Beta Exercise	10 minutes
Model for Effective Business Writing	10 minutes
Learning Activity 10. Personal Case Scenario	10 minutes
Plan Your Writing Content	15 minutes
BREAK	**10 minutes**
Learning Activity 11. Document Planning Mind Map	20 minutes
Brainstorm . . . Brainstorming!	10 minutes
Five Cs of Effective Communication	5 minutes
Learning Activity 12. Five Cs	10 minutes
BREAK	**10 minutes**
Learning Activity 18. Identify Your Reader's Needs	10 minutes
Most Commonly Forgotten Communication Factors	5 minutes
Learning Activity 19. Draft Your Message	15 minutes
Reflection and Action Plan	10 minutes
Session Summary and Q&A	5 minutes
TOTAL	**240 Minutes (4 Hours)**

Considerations for the Virtual Environment

Conducting a workshop in a virtual format is often necessary to provide benefits of time and location flexibility as well as to account for cost. Unfortunately, this modality also brings the risk of some challenges, such as technology limitations, distracted learners, a lack of nonverbal cues, and the highly beneficial informal, but relevant, sidebar conversations that take place among learners in a shared space with a shared interest. When considering conducting a workshop in a virtual format, the following recommendations may help minimize some of these risks:

- To keep participants engaged, ensure that you maintain a high level of energy and frequently solicit input, both verbal and through the use of the technology tools throughout the duration of the workshop.

- Actively seek frequent feedback from participants to gauge their understanding.

- Use the video feature as much as possible so participants can see that they have an instructor who is working with them and not just sharing static slides on a screen.

- Encourage participants to use their video features when speaking to help better engage with one another.

- See chapter 4 for suggestions on how this content can be grouped into sessions that are shorter or topic specific.

Preparation

While all facilitation sessions require preparation, the success of a virtual session is even more dependent on how carefully the facilitator prepares and the completion of a thorough and deliberate setup. The following checklists have been provided to help you ensure a smooth and effective workshop delivery. Please note, these checklists have been created with a WebEx environment in mind. As technologies and platforms can differ, you are encouraged to modify these recommendations based on the specific needs of your delivery.

Pre-Workshop—Facilitator Checklist

✓	TASK	SUGGESTED TIMEFRAME
	Upload presentation files	One week prior to session.
	Review the facilitator guide and any other course materials.	Ideally, one week prior to the start of the session, but no later than 72 hours in advance.

✓	TASK	SUGGESTED TIMEFRAME
	Validate the final participant list.	Ideally, one week prior to the start of the session, but no later than 72 hours in advance.
	Send a welcome email to participants. Let them know you are looking forward to the class, and include reminders to complete any necessary prework and to verify connection and compatibility. Highlight the fact that this is designed to be an interactive workshop, which means that they may be asked to share their screen and video camera during the sessions so may want to ensure appropriate and respectful appearance and attire. An addition, they will be asked to interact with others in the session frequently and will need to minimize any external distractions to get the most favorable learning experience from the course.	One week prior to the session.
	Distribute handouts and any other documents that will used in class. Refer to chapter 13 for information on how to access and use the supplemental materials provided for this workshop.	If sending hard copies, ensure that they are sent with plenty of time for delivery. If sending electronically (for example through email or a Dropbox link) share at least 72 hours in advance.
	Create polls and breakout rooms.	At least 72 hours before the session.
	Ensure you're familiar with how the interactivity functionality within your presentation platform works. You need to be able to explain this to participants. You may also want to create a short cheat sheet that you can use to demonstrate these functions as you welcome participants to the session. This is particularly important if you are conducting a session for participants from multiple organizations.	At least 72 hours before the session.

Create Polls

Create this poll before the start of the workshop. Ensure that the poll is set to share responses with all participants.

✓	LOCATION	POLL RESPONSES
	Slide 2 (Objectives)	• Identify the most common barriers of organizational communication. • Examine organizational dynamics to assess the best approach for communicating in challenging situations. • Explain the Five Cs of Effective Communication (clear, concise, complete, correct, and considerate). • Draft a message that uses all Five Cs.

Create Breakout Rooms

Create these breakout rooms before the start of the workshop.

✓	ROOM DESCRIPTION	NOTES
	Create enough breakout rooms that the participants can be split into groups of five or fewer. Randomly assign each participant to a room so that the groups are roughly equal in number. Label rooms: • Room 1 • Room 2 • Room 3 • Room 4 • and so on Create a list of who has been assigned to each room that you can display onscreen at the start of the activity.	You will use these breakout rooms for the following activities: • Brainstorm. . . Brainstorming! • Learning Activity 12. The Five Cs • Learning Activity 18. Identifying Your Readers' Needs

✓	ROOM DESCRIPTION	NOTES
	Create enough breakout rooms to accommodate breaking the group up into pairs. For example, if you have 20 participants, you will need 10 breakout rooms. Randomly assign each participant to a room. Label rooms: • Pair 1 • Pair 2 • Pair 3 • Pair 4 • and so on Create a list of who has been assigned to each room that you can display onscreen at the start of the activity.	You will use these breakout rooms for the following activity: • Learning Activity 19. Draft Your Message

Half-Day Workshop Agenda

Half Day (8 a.m. to 12 p.m.)

TIMING	SLIDES	ACTIVITIES/NOTES/CONSIDERATIONS
8 a.m. (10 min)	Slide 1 ATD Workshop Effective Communication Skills	**Welcome and Introduction** Briefly welcome the participants and introduce yourself. Provide a quick overview of the functionality and interactivity elements that will be used during the session (e.g., polls, chat, whiteboard, breakout sessions). A sample functionality overview has been provided. This sample is specific to the WebEx environment. Ensure that participants are aware that they may be asked to share their screens or cameras as part of the exercises and activities during the workshop.

TIMING	SLIDES	ACTIVITIES/NOTES/CONSIDERATIONS
8:10 a.m. (10 min)	Slide 2c **Two-Day Workshop Objectives** • Identify the most common barriers of communication. • Explain the Five Cs of Effective Communication. • Assess your listening skills. • Explain and practice active listening skills. • Determine the best way to get your point across. • Examine situational dynamics to assess the best approach for communicating in challenging situations. • Apply effective principles for face-to-face, written, and virtual scenarios.	**Learning Activity 1. Objective Decision** • **Handout 1c. Objective Decision** • **Poll: Objectives** This activity provides an innovative way to facilitate the discussion about session objectives rather than simply reading them to the participants. Ask participants to follow the instructions in the handout. When they are finished ask them to use the poll to select the objective that corresponds to the one they highlighted. Share poll results with all.
8:20 a.m. (5 min)	Slide 3 **Ground Rules and Expectations** • Participate! • Explore new ideas • Have fun • "Vegas rule" • What else?	**Ground Rules and Expectations** Facilitate a discussion about ground rules and expectations for the course. Adjust times as needed for starting and ending and breaks. It is important to establish a positive learning environment. Ask participants to give you a green check if they are in agreement with the ground rules for the session.
8:25 a.m. (50 min)	Slide 48 **Alpha Beta Exercise** Exercise rules: • Solve a simple, analytical problem. • Communicate in writing only. • No oral communication permitted. • Deliver your messages through chat. • When you believe you have solved the problem, Alpha or Beta will raise a hand and I will check your answer.	**Learning Activity 9. Alpha Beta Exercise** • **Handout 14. Alpha Beta Exercise** This activity seems more complicated than it is, so be sure to use the full facilitation process and follow instructions in the learning activity. It is a silent activity, so once you explain the directions all participant communication will be done in writing. Show Slide 48 and present the rules for this exercise. Encourage participants to reference the handout during the activity. (Slide 1 of 4)

TIMING	SLIDES	ACTIVITIES/NOTES/CONSIDERATIONS
	Slide 49 Alpha Beta Exercise Communication process: • Only written communication allowed • All communication is sent by direct chat to the messenger for distribution. (Do not send to "all participants.") • Improperly addressed mail will be returned or destroyed	**Learning Activity 9. Alpha Beta Exercise** • **Handout 14. Alpha Beta Exercise** Show Slide 49 and present the rules for the communication process that is used in this exercise. It's important that the organizational hierarchy is strictly followed. Encourage participants to reference the handout during the activity. (Slide 2 of 4)
	Slide 50 Alpha Beta Exercise Addressing Your Messages TO: [recipient] (for example, Alpha) FROM: [sender] (for example, Beta) ✕ Note: The messenger will check your mail to ensure it is properly addressed. If not addressed correctly, your messages may be returned to you or lost in cyberspace.	**Learning Activity 9. Alpha Beta Exercise** • **Handout 14. Alpha Beta Exercise** Show Slide 50 and present the format participants will use to send messages in this exercise. Encourage participants to reference the handout during the activity. (Slide 3 of 4)
9:15 a.m. (10 min)	Slide 52 10-Minute Break	**BREAK** Encourage participants to get up and move around. Emphasize that they should try to look away from their computers or phones during the break if possible.
9:25 a.m. (10 min)	Slide 51 Debrief and Discussion How is this experience similar to what really occurs in the workplace?	**Learning Activity 9. Alpha Beta Exercise** • **Handout 14. Alpha Beta Exercise** This activity has the potential to drive a very rich discussion. Debrief the questions using any method you wish (e.g., the chat pane or raise hand). Encourage participants to record their insights on the handout. (Slide 4 of 4)

TIMING	SLIDES	ACTIVITIES/NOTES/CONSIDERATIONS
	Slide 53 Whiteboard What makes "good" business writing?	**Whiteboard Discussion** Write: "What makes good business writing?" on the whiteboard. Ask participants to either raise their hand or reply in chat. Capture their ideas on the whiteboard.
9:35 a.m. (10 min)	Slide 54 Model for Effective Business Writing	**Model for Effective Business Writing** • **Handout 15. Model for Effective Business Writing** Introduce the model for effective business writing and summarize the steps. Encourage participants to follow along on slide 54 or Handout 15.
9:45 a.m. (10 min)	Slide 80 Personal Case Scenario Think about one, two, or three pieces of recent or current business communication that you can use to review, prepare, or evaluate throughout the day.	**Learning Activity 10. Personal Case Scenario** • **Handout 16. Personal Case Scenario Worksheet** Ask participants to think about one, two, or three recent or current business communications they can use to review, prepare, or evaluate throughout the day.
9:55 a.m. (15 min)	Slide 55 Planning Your Writing Content Brainstorming Questions • What is the purpose? • Who is your audience? • What are their needs? • What are your expectations (and theirs)? • What is the core content for your message?	**Plan Your Writing Content** Review the brainstorming questions on Slide 55, and explain how they can be used in the mind mapping technique.

TIMING	SLIDES	ACTIVITIES/NOTES/CONSIDERATIONS
	Slide 56 Whiteboard Mind Mapping	**Demonstrate the Development of a Mind Map** Each main limb of the map is used for building on the original concept and branching out by adding relevant ideas to the main concept: Choose a topic to place in the center of the map (for example, an upcoming event). • Label the first limb "audience" and then add additional branches for each stakeholder member identified. • Label the next limb "need" and add branches with answers in that category. • Label another "expectations" and add branches. • Label another "content" and add branches.
10:10 a.m. (10 min)	Slide 52 10-Minute Break	**BREAK** Encourage participants to get up and move around. Emphasize that they should look away from their computers or phones during the break if possible.
10:20 a.m. (20 min)	Slide 57 Document Planning Mind Map Planning to write: • Purpose? • Audience? • Needs? • Expectations? • Core message?	**Learning Activity 11. Document Planning Mind Map** • **Handout 17. Mind Map: Plan Your Content** Now it is your participants' turn. Instruct them to choose a personal case scenario from Handout 16 and map all content planning considerations. Ask participants to give you a green checkmark when they have completed their maps. Debrief the questions using any method you wish (e.g., chat pane or raise hand).

TIMING	SLIDES	ACTIVITIES/NOTES/CONSIDERATIONS
10:40 a.m. (10 min)	Slide 59 Brainstorm... Brainstorming!	**Brainstorm . . . Brainstorming!** • **Handout 18. Brainstorm Other Brainstorming Methods** • **Breakout Room** Inform participants that they have been randomly broken into small groups for this learning activity. Show the list of participant assignments on the screen. Ask participants to join their assigned breakout rooms to brainstorm other brainstorming techniques besides mind mapping. Instruct them to record their insights on the handouts, which also include best practices for productive brainstorming. Bring everyone back to the main room and debrief using any method you wish (e.g., chat pane or raise hand). Capture the responses on the whiteboard.
10:50 a.m. (5 min)	Slide 60 Five Cs of Effective Communication • Clear • Concise • Complete • Correct • Considerate	**Five Cs of Effective Communication** • **Handout 19. Five Cs of Effective Communication** Present the Five Cs of Effective Communication. Participants can follow along and take additional notes on the handout.
10:55 a.m. (10 min)	Slide 61 Whiteboard Which of the Five Cs is omitted and why?	**Learning Activity 12. The Five Cs** • **Whiteboard** • **Handout 19. Five Cs of Effective Communication** • **Breakout Room** Follow the facilitation instructions in Learning Activity 12. Ask participants to work in their assigned breakout rooms to identify communication pitfalls. Display the list of groups on the screen. Bring everyone back to the main room and debrief using any method you wish (e.g., chat pane or raise hand). Capture all responses on the whiteboard.

TIMING	SLIDES	ACTIVITIES/NOTES/CONSIDERATIONS
11:05 a.m. (10 min)	Slide 58 10-Minute Break	**BREAK** Encourage participants to get up and move around. Emphasize that they should try to look away from their computers or phones during the break if possible.
11:15 a.m. (10 min)	Slide 69 Identifying Your Reader's Needs What is your intent versus what they need to hear? Needs / Wants	**Learning Activity 18. Identify Your Reader's Needs** • **Handout 25. The Wants and Needs of Your Reader** • **Breakout Room** Use your method of choice to facilitate a discussion around the reader's wants and needs. Have participants begin by considering what they want and need as readers and then extrapolate to their audience. This conversation is very helpful for encouraging them to carefully consider and plan the content of their written messages. Your audience is looking to answer these questions: • What is this about, and does it matter to me? • What do I have to do now, and when is it due? • What data do I need to know from this? • How does this make me feel? • Can I skip this altogether? Use the breakout rooms to allow groups to complete the worksheet in the handout. After 7–8 minutes, bring everyone back and ask for volunteers to share their responses. Capture their answers in appropriate column on the screen. Debrief the questions using any method you wish (e.g., chat pane or raise hand).
11:25 a.m. (5 min)	Slide 81 Debrief and Discussion What are the most commonly forgotten communication factors?	**Most Commonly Forgotten Communication Factors** It is helpful to discuss the Five Cs from a big-picture perspective. Use Slide 81 as a focal point for a wrap-up conversation before participants draft a document.

TIMING	SLIDES	ACTIVITIES/NOTES/CONSIDERATIONS
11:30 a.m. (15 min)	Slide 70 Draft Your Message Draft the Message Five Cs · Clear · Concise · Complete · Considerate · Correct	**Learning Activity 19. Draft Your Message** • **Handout 26. Draft Your Message** • **Breakout Room** This activity helps participants practice drafting a document that considers the needs of the reader and conforms to the Five Cs (clear, concise, complete, correct, and considerate). Break participants into pairs and direct them to their preassigned breakout rooms to share their thoughts and provide each other feedback. Show the list of assignments to the screen. Follow the facilitation instructions in Learning Activity 19. After 10–12 minutes, bring everyone back and ask for volunteers to share their responses with the class. Debrief using any method you wish (e.g., chat pane or raise hand).
11:45 a.m. (10 min)	Slide 74 Reflection and Action Plan What behaviors will you… • Start? • Stop? • Continue?	**Reflection and Action Plan** • **Handout 27. Reflection and Action Plan** Ask: "What will you do differently as a result of this class?" Solicit input using any method you wish (e.g., chat pane or raise hand). Capture any comments on the whiteboard. Allow participants time to reflect and complete the action plan. This will help them solidify what they've learned.
11:55 a.m. (5 min) End 12 p.m.	Slide 75 Summary	**Session Summary and Q&A** Facilitate a discussion and solicit feedback about the best take-aways from the course. Capture responses on the whiteboard.

What to Do Next

- Determine the training schedule; confirm which platform you're going to use and familiarize yourself with it.

- Identify and invite participants.

- Inform participants about and distribute any prework. Consider using self-assessment instruments (such as Assessment 1. Listening Behavior Assessment or Assessment 2. Communication Style Inventory).

- Review the workshop objectives, activities, and handouts to plan the content you will use.

- Prepare the participant materials and any activity-related extras for electronic distribution. Refer to chapter 13 for information on how to access and use the included supplemental materials.

- Prepare yourself both emotionally and physically. Make sure you've taken care of any scheduling conflicts or personal challenges (as best you can), so you can be fully present to facilitate the class.

- Get a good night's sleep before you facilitate the workshop so you have the energy and focus to deliver a great class!

Chapter 4

Customizing the Communication Skills Workshop

What's in This Chapter

- Ideas for creating a communication skills workshop
- Creative approaches for developing Lunch & Learn seminars
- Suggestions for designing theme-based workshops

Many organizations find it difficult to have employees away from their day-to-day responsibilities for an entire day or two, even if it requires no travel and is for professional and skill development. As a result, you may need to adapt your workshop to the scheduling needs of the organization. Additionally, organizations often prefer to select the content to match the needs of the employees attending the training. Your training needs analysis will help you prioritize and select the content and activities of highest value for your participants. For more on needs analysis, see chapter 5.

The materials in this book are designed to meet a variety of training needs. They cover a range of topics related to communication skills training and can be offered in many timeframes and formats. Although lengthy immersion in a learning environment can enhance and increase the depth of learning experiences, the challenges of the workplace sometimes demand that training be done in small doses.

By using the expertly designed learning content and activities provided here as a foundation, you can modify and adapt the learning experience by customizing the content and activities, the workshop format, and the delivery with technology.

Customizing the Content and Activities

As mentioned in the introduction of this book, your level of expertise with training facilitation and communication skills will determine how much customization you should do with the workshops presented here. If you are new to both training and the topic, you'll want to follow the workshops as closely as possible. If you are a new trainer but an expert in communication skills, use the outline and materials as designed but feel free to include relevant materials you have developed. And, finally, if you are an expert facilitator, feel free to adapt the agenda and materials as you see fit. Add any new materials you have developed to augment the learning. Or you can simply incorporate the learning activities, assessments, handouts, and tools into your own agenda. As you become more confident with the topic and facilitation, you will be able to introduce more of your own personal style into the workshop. You will also be better able to tailor the workshops to specific organizational needs and business imperatives.

In addition to your level of expertise, your depth of experience with creating and delivering courses in a virtual environment will significantly impact your ability to effectively customize the content. If you are not experienced in virtual training facilitation, it is recommended that you seek the support of an experienced peer or a virtual training producer to support the development and delivery of your workshop.

When customizing for a virtual delivery, several unique factors must be considered:

- **Comfort level with the delivery platform.** A successful virtual delivery can be completely derailed if the facilitator or participants are unable to interact as planned. Your level of comfort and experience with the platform and its functionalities must allow you to not only navigate it yourself, but also to ensure that your participants can use it successfully. Any customization should be rehearsed from both a facilitator and participant viewpoint.

- **Content and activity suitability.** Virtual deliveries allow for significant flexibility in location and timing, but they also inhibit some of the face-to-face interactions and group cohesiveness that you can achieve in a classroom setting. These interactions tend to encourage participation and a deeper understanding of the content. When customizing this content for a virtual delivery, it is important that you consider the goals of the activity or content and then evaluate if it will have the same impact with the inherent limitations of the modality.

- **Timing.** Many of the discussions and other activities that move quite quickly in a classroom setting may take longer in a virtual setting. For example, interactions that require participants to use the chat feature or move in and out of breakout rooms can increase the total time needed for the activity. You will also need to factor in time for screen breaks. Participants in a virtual setting should be encouraged to take a brief break to move around and look away from their screens approximately every 45–60 minutes if possible.

- **Encouraging participation.** As you customize content, it is important to add in reminders for participants to interact (every three to five minutes, if possible). Use verbal cues, such as *put your thoughts into the chat window, vote on the poll that just popped up, and use the annotation tool to make your mark on the slide.*

Here are some ways to introduce new elements into your training workshop:

- **Explore variations in learning activities.** Many of the learning activities in this book include ideas for variations. Try out some of these alternatives to see if any resonate with your facilitation style and your participants' preferences. Table 4-1 provides a list of learning activities and some specific considerations for the virtual format.

- **Use the book's bonus materials.** To help provide variety and enable flexibility in your workshops, we have included several bonus learning activities and assessments. Table 4-2 shows a list of bonus materials that are not used in the half-, one-, or two-day workshop agendas but may can be included to customize the workshop experience.

Table 4-1. Learning Activities

ACTIVITY		CONSIDERATIONS
1.	Objective Decision	May be conducted as a poll in the virtual setting.
2.	The Most Difficult Person	This activity has been modified for use in the virtual setting.
3.	Identify the Noise	Depending on the number of participants, this activity may require the use of breakout rooms.
4.	Impression Improv	This activity has been modified for use in the virtual setting. Please note that it requires video capabilities for the facilitator and participants.
5.	Surgical Analysis of Your Story	
6.	Listening Is More Than Hearing	This activity has been modified for use in the virtual setting. Please note that it requires screen sharing or video and direct messaging capabilities for the facilitator and participants.
7.	Listening Stick (Part 1)	This activity has been modified for use in the virtual setting. Please note that this activity requires the use of breakout rooms, and video capability for participants is recommended.

ACTIVITY	CONSIDERATIONS
8. Listening Stick (Part 2)	This activity has been modified for use in the virtual setting. Please note that this activity requires the use of breakout rooms, and video capability for participants is recommended.
9. Alpha Beta Exercise	This activity has been modified for use in the virtual setting. Please note that this activity requires use of the direct message chat functions.
10. Personal Case Scenario	This activity is completed by each participant individually and therefore may be assigned as prework or homework.
11. Document Planning Mind Map	You will use the whiteboard or screenshare functions to demonstrate the development of a mind map in this activity.
12. Five Cs	This activity has been modified for use in the virtual setting. The whiteboard and breakout rooms are used for this activity.
13. Clear Communication	This activity requires the use of breakout rooms.
14. Concise Communication	This activity requires the use of breakout rooms.
15. Complete Communication	This activity requires the use of breakout rooms.
16. Correct Communication	This activity requires the use of breakout rooms.
17. Considerate Communication: Circles of Influence	The whiteboard function is used in place of a flipchart for this activity.
18. Identify Your Reader's Needs	This activity requires the use of breakout rooms.
19. Draft Your Message	This activity requires the use of breakout rooms.

Table 4-2. Bonus Learning Materials

TYPE	TOPIC	CONSIDERATIONS
Learning Activities	20. Effective Virtual Teams (Part 1)	.
	21. Effective Virtual Teams (Part 2)	
	22. 10 Questions About Conflict	This activity may be conducted as a large group or in smaller groups using breakout rooms.
	23. Choices	This activity may be suited to a virtual delivery using the chat feature to get participant input.

TYPE	TOPIC	CONSIDERATIONS
Learner Assessments	2. Communication Style Inventory	This assessment may be assigned as pre-, post-, or homework and then used as a discussion topic either in a large group or smaller groups. Divide the groups based on the traits or behaviors you want to address or emphasize.
	5. Interpersonal Skills	This assessment is conducted independently. Results may also be used to guide a discussion around perception and self-awareness.
	8. Nonverbal Communication Self-Assessment	This assessment is conducted independently. Results may also be used to guide a discussion around self-awareness and ability to adjust to the needs of the listener.
	9. Skills Application Reflection	This assessment is conducted independently. Results may be used as a closing discussion to recap the topics that were most useful to participants.
	10. Skills Mastery Assessment	This assessment is conducted independently. Results may be used as a closing discussion to recap the topics that were most useful to participants.
Facilitator Assessments	3. Course Evaluation	This assessment may be conducted by individuals or setup as a series of poll questions.
	4. Facilitator Competencies	This assessment may be conducted by individuals or be set up as a series of poll questions.
	6. Learning Needs Assessment Sheet	This assessment is conducted by the facilitator with stakeholders in advance.
	7. Needs Analysis Discussion Form	This assessment is conducted by the facilitator with stakeholders in advance.

Customizing the Workshop Format

Using the content from the two-day workshop (chapter 1), you can adapt the workshop format to build a series of two-hour workshops, lunchtime seminars, or thematic workshops.

Communication Skills Workshop Series

To address the need to provide shorter training segments, Table 4-3 breaks down the content into a series of eight two-hour workshops. These workshops can be offered on a daily, weekly, biweekly, or monthly basis, depending on the organization's scheduling needs. Consider using Assessment 9: Skills Application Reflection or Assessment 10: Skills Mastery Assessment to help solidify what content to include in the series. Each of these instruments provides a way to help participants quickly bring what they've learned back to the workplace.

Table 4-3. Communication Skills Workshop Series

SESSION	WORKSHOP TOPICS
1	• Communication Process • Identify the Noise • Communication Pie • Impression Improv
2	• Vocal Tone and Word Emphasis • Congruent and Incongruent Communication • The Emotional and Rational Brain • Strategies for Gaining Emotional Control
3	• Communication Awareness Model • Five Steps to Effective Communication • Surgical Analysis of Your Story • Personal Case Scenario
4	• Typical Listening • Listening Stick (Part 1) • Barriers to Listening
5	• Principles of Active Listening • Listening Stick (Part 2)
6	• Alpha Beta Communication • Model for Effective Business Writing • Planning Your Writing Content
7	• Five Cs of Effective Communication • Clear, Concise, Complete, Correct, Considerate
8	• Circles of Communication Influence • Identifying Your Reader's Needs • Drafting Your Message and Designing Your Document

Small Bites—Lunch & Learn Seminars

Sometimes small means big impact. Table 4-4 shows topics that could be delivered effectively in one-hour sessions. The key to doing these bite-sized chunks successfully is to have a clear design with the right amount of content. Trying to cram in too much content can make a seminar seem shallow and rushed. Ask yourself the key question when creating a session of this size: What is one key concept I would like the participants to remember after this workshop?

Table 4-4. Lunch & Learn Seminars

TOPICS FOR ONE-HOUR LUNCHTIME SEMINARS
• Communication Process • Identify the Noise
• Communication Pie • Impression Improv
• Impact of Body Language • Congruent and Incongruent Communication
• Role of Emotion in Communication • Symptoms of Fear or Anger
• Emotional and Rational Brain • Strategies for Gaining Emotional Control
• Communication Awareness Model • Five Steps to Effective Communication • Surgical Analysis of Your Story
• Basic Listening • Listening Stick (Part 1)
• Principles of Active Listening • Listening Stick (Part 2) • Barriers to Listening
• Communicating in Writing • Alpha Beta Communication
• Model for Effective Business Writing • Planning Your Writing
• Five Cs of Effective Communication • Clear, Concise, Complete, Correct, Considerate
• Circles of Communication Influence • Identifying Your Reader's Needs
• Drafting Your Message and Designing Your Document • Clear, Concise, Complete, Correct, Considerate

Theme-Based Workshops

Communication is a topic that permeates most other workplace learning topics. Table 4-5 shows five major communication skill themes around which you can create training: leadership, listening, virtual teams, business writing, and cultural considerations. Mix and match the content topics and activities in the second column to create a workshop focused on key aspects of communication skills training.

Table 4-5. Theme-Based Workshops

THEME	WORKSHOP TOPICS
Leadership	• Communication Process • Alpha Beta Exercise • Identify the Noise • Communication Pie • Impression Improv • Emotional and Rational Brain • Strategies for Gaining Emotional Control • Choices Activity
Listening Skills	• Typical Listening • Listening Stick (Part 1) • Barriers to Listening • Principles of Active Listening • Listening Stick (Part 2) • Impact of Body Language • Congruent and Incongruent Communication • Emotional and Rational Brain • Strategies for Gaining Emotional Control • Nonverbal Communication Self-Assessment
Virtual Teams	• Communication Awareness Model • Five Steps to Effective Communication • Surgical Analysis of Your Story • Personal Case Scenario • Effective Virtual Teams (Parts 1 and 2) • Interpersonal Skills Assessment
Business Writing	• Communicating in Writing • Alpha Beta Communication • Five Cs of Effective Communication • Clear, Concise, Complete, Correct, Considerate • Model for Effective Business Writing • Planning Your Writing • Identifying Your Reader's Needs • Drafting Your Message and Designing Your Document

THEME	WORKSHOP TOPICS
Cultural Considerations	• Circles of Influence • Barriers to Listening • Impact of Body Language • Congruent and Incongruent Communication • 10 Questions About Conflict

Pay Attention to Copyright

Copyright law is a sticky, complex area that is beyond the scope of this book to address in detail. For legal advice, consult your legal department.

However, it's very important to note a few things about copyright, fair use, and intellectual property:

- Just because you found an image, article, music, or video online doesn't mean that you can use it in training without permission. Make sure you obtain permission from the copyright owner before you use it (sometimes the copyright owner is not obvious and you will need to do some research).

- Fair use is pretty limited. Although most fair use allows an educational exception, that does not include corporate or organizational training. Other exceptions relate to how much material relative to the original was used, the nature of the original work (creative work generally has more protection), and the effect on the market for the original (Swindling and Partridge 2008). Once again, your best bet is to get written permission.

- Just because something doesn't have a copyright notice on it doesn't mean that it isn't copyright protected. All original material is protected under copyright law as soon as it is published or created.

Don't despair. Plenty of online sources of images, videos, text, and so forth exist that you can use for free or for a minimal fee. Just search on the terms "copyright free" or "open source." Another place to look is Wikimedia Commons, which has millions of freely usable media files. For more information about how copyright law affects your use of materials in this volume, please see Chapter 13 on how to use the online materials and downloads.

The Bare Minimum

With any of these customization options, always keep in mind the essentials of training design (chapter 6) and delivery (chapter 7). At a bare minimum, remember to:

- **Prepare, prepare, prepare.** Set up the platform (such as polls and breakout rooms), the handouts, and the equipment. Make sure to familiarize yourself with the platform, content, materials, timing, and equipment. Practice can only make you a better facilitator. The more comfortable you feel, the more open and relaxed you will be for your participants.

- **Start well.** The beginning of a session is a crucial time in the workshop dynamic. How the participants respond to you, the facilitator, can set the mood for the rest of the workshop. Log in to the platform and open the room at least 30 minutes before the session starts. Make sure to address any problems before the participants arrive so you can be available to welcome them. Ask simple questions while they are settling in to start building rapport. After introducing yourself, provide an activity in which participants can meet one another and get comfortable with the platform's features. Remind participants to mute themselves when not speaking so everyone can hear clearly.

- **Don't lecture too long!** Adult learners like to have fun and participate in interactive learning opportunities. Be sure to vary the learning and teaching method regularly to keep the pace active and engaging during an online class (industry best practices recommend changing topic or activity every eight to 10 minutes). Use the interactivity features (such as checkmarks, chat, whiteboard, and emojis) often to ensure participants stay engaged.

- **End strong.** Providing time for participants to reflect and create an action plan at the end of a module or session will help solidify learning. Don't skip this opportunity to encourage them to take action on something they have learned. Use the action plan worksheet (Handouts 13 and 27) so they can write down their goals. Or consider using the instruments on skills application and skills mastery (Assessments 9 and 10, respectively).

What to Do Next

- When customizing a workshop, it is important to have a clear understanding of the learning objectives. Conduct a needs analysis to identify the gap between what the organization needs and what the employees are able to do, and then determine how best to bridge that gap. At a minimum, you should identify who wants the training, how the results will be defined, why the training is being requested now, and what the budget is. Chapter 5 provides more guidance on identifying training needs.

- Modify or add your own content to an existing agenda from the first three chapters or create your own agenda using the learning support documents included in this book.

There is no one best way to flow communications skills content, but you must ensure that the topics build on one another and that you solidly connect the concepts and ideas to get the most out of the learning opportunity.

- Incorporate interactive practice activities into the workshop.

- Compile and review any learning activities, handouts, and slides you will use for the session.

- Build a detailed plan for preparing for the session, including scheduling, creating breakout rooms, sending invitations, generating teaching notes, and planning out your timeline.

SECTION II

ESSENTIALS OF EFFECTIVE COMMUNICATION SKILLS TRAINING

Chapter 5

Identifying Needs for Communication Skills Training

What's in This Chapter

- Discovering the purpose of needs analysis
- Introducing some data-gathering methods
- Determining the bare minimum needed to deliver training

Ideally, you should always carry out a needs analysis before designing and creating a workshop to address a performance gap. The cost of *not* identifying and carefully considering the performance requirement can be high: wasted training dollars, unhappy staff going to boring or useless sessions, increased disengagement of employees, and so forth. But the world of training is rarely ideal, and the existence of this book, which essentially provides a workshop in a box, is testament to that. This chapter describes the essential theory and techniques for a complete needs analysis to provide the fundamentals of the process and how it fits into designing learning. However, because the decision to train may already be out of your hands, the last part of this chapter provides a bare-bones list of things you need to know to train effectively even if someone just handed you this book and told you to put on a workshop.

Why Needs Analysis?

In short, as a trainer, learning professional, performance consultant, or whatever job title you hold, your role is to ensure that the employees of your organization know how to do the work that will make the organization succeed. That means you must first identify the skills, knowledge, and abilities that the employees need for optimal performance and then determine where these are lacking in the employee population to bridge that gap. A training needs analysis helps you do this (see Figure 5-1). Methods to identify this information include strategic needs analysis, structured interviews, focus groups, and surveys.

Strategic Needs Analysis

An analysis of future directions usually identifies emerging issues and trends with a major potential effect on a business and its customers over a two- to three-year period. The analysis helps a business develop goals and programs that proactively anticipate and position the organization to influence the future.

Figure 5-1. Introducing the ADDIE Model

A needs analysis is the first step in the classic instructional design model called ADDIE, which is named after its steps: analysis, design, development, implementation, and evaluation. Roughly speaking, the tasks involved in ADDIE are:

1. **Analysis:** Gather data about organizational and individual needs as well as the gap between the goals the organization means to accomplish and the skills and knowledge needed to accomplish those goals.

2. **Design:** Identify and plan the topics and sequence of learning to accomplish the desired learning.

3. **Development:** Create the components of the learning event, such as learning activities and materials.

4. **Implementation:** Put on the learning event or launch the learning materials.

5. **Evaluation:** Gather data to determine the outcome of the learning to improve future iterations of the learning, enhance materials and facilitation, and justify budget decisions.

Instructional design models such as ADDIE are a systematic approach to developing learning and could also be viewed as a project management framework for the project phases involved in creating learning events.

To conduct such an analysis, organizations look at issues such as expected changes within the business (for example, technology and professional requirements) and expected changes outside the company (for example, the economy, demographics, politics, and the environment).

Results of an analysis provide a rationale for developing company and departmental goals and for making policy and budgetary decisions. From the analysis comes a summary of key change dynamics that will affect the business.

These questions often are asked in strategic needs analysis:

- What information did previous organizational analyses impart?
- Are those issues and trends still relevant?
- Do the results point to what may need to be done differently in the future?
- How has the organization performed in achieving results?
- What is the present workforce like?
- How will it change or need to change?
- What does the organization know about future changes in customer needs?
- Are customer surveys conducted, and if so, what do they reveal?
- How might the organization have to change to serve customers better?
- Is the company's organizational structure working to achieve results?
- What are the strengths and limitations of the company?
- What are the opportunities for positive change?
- What do competitors do or say that might have implications for the organization?
- What are the most important opportunities for the future?
- What are the biggest problems?
- Is the organization in a competitive marketplace?
- How does the organization compare with competitors?
- The results can be summarized in a SWOT analysis model (strengths, weaknesses, opportunities, threats—see Figure 5-2). Action plans are then developed to increase the strengths, overcome the weaknesses, plan for the opportunities, and decrease the threats.

Figure 5-2. SWOT Analysis Model

	STRENGTHS	WEAKNESSES
INTERNAL		
	OPPORTUNITIES	THREATS
EXTERNAL		

Structured Interviews

Start structured interviews as high up in the organization as you can go, with the CEO if possible. Make sure that you include input from human resource personnel and line or operations managers and supervisors. Managers and supervisors will want to tell you what they have seen and what they consider the most pressing issues in the organization. Use Assessment 6: Learning Needs Assessment Sheet to capture your notes from the interviews.

Focus Groups

Focus groups can be set up to give people opportunities to brainstorm ideas about issues in the organization and to realize the potential of team involvement. One comment may spark another and so on. Focus groups should begin with questions that you prepare. It is important to record the responses and comments on a flipchart so everyone can see them. If that is not possible, you may simply take notes. Results of the sessions should be compiled. A needs analysis discussion form (Assessment 7) is provided in chapter 11 to help focus group members prepare for the discussion.

Surveys

Surveys, whether paper- or web-based, gather information from a large or geographically dispersed group of employees. The advantages of surveys are speed of data collection, objectivity, repeatability, and ease of analysis.

A Note From the Author

When conducting a needs analysis around communication skills, it is important to keep in mind the various aspects of communication challenges. Here is a list of questions to ask to help guide your analysis:

- Does the organizational culture set a tone for open and honest communication?
- Has the organization conducted many employee surveys without taking action on the results?
- Are the managers skilled in handling difficult conversations?
- Do employees have a process or vehicle to communicate their concerns?

Individual Learning Needs Analysis

While identifying organizational learning needs is critical to making the best use of an organization's training budget, analyzing individual learning needs is also important. Understanding the training group's current skills and knowledge can help to focus the training on those areas that require most work—this also helps to avoid going over what the individuals already know, thus wasting their time, or losing them by jumping in at too advanced a level. In addition, individual learning needs analysis can uncover unfavorable attitudes about training that trainers will be better able to address if they are prepared for them. For example, some learners may see the training as a waste of time, as an interruption to their normal work, or as a sign of potentially frightening organizational change.

Many of the same methods used to gather data for organizational learning needs are used for individual learning needs analysis. Analyzing employee learning needs should be carried out in a thoughtful, sensitive, and inclusive manner. Here are potential pitfalls to avoid:

- **Don't analyze needs you can't meet.** Training needs analysis raises expectations. It sends a message to employees that the organization expects them to be competent in particular areas.

- **Involve employees directly.** Sometimes employees don't see a value in participating in training. In assessing needs, trainers need to prepare employees to buy into the training. Asking useful questions and listening carefully to stated needs are excellent methods for accomplishing both of those goals. Ask these questions: "To what degree would you like to learn how to do [X] more effectively?" and "To what degree would you seriously consider participating in training to improve your competency in [X]?"

- **Make the identified needs an obvious part of your training design.** Trainees should be able to see that they have influenced the content and emphasis of the training session. A good practice is briefly to summarize the local trends discovered in the training needs analysis when you introduce the goals of the session.

- **Don't think of training as a "magic bullet."** Sometimes a given employee needs coaching, counseling, or consulting, which is best carried out one on one and customized to the individual and the situation. Still other times, the problem is caused by equipment or processes that need upgrading, not people who need training.

The Bare Minimum

As noted, in an ideal world, you would have gathered all this data about the needs of the organization and the employees and determined that training was the right way to connect those dots. However, even if the decision to put on this workshop has already been made, you still need a bare minimum of information to be successful:

- **Who is your project sponsor (who wants to do this, provides the budget, and so on)?** In fact, if you don't have a project sponsor, *stop* the project. Lack of a project sponsor indicates that the project isn't important to the business. Optimally, the project sponsor should come from the business side of the organization. If the project sponsor is the head of training, then the mentality behind the training—"build it and they will come"—is likely wrong. Even compliance training should have a functional sponsor.

- **What does the sponsor want the learners to be able to do when they are done with training?** How does the sponsor define measures of success? Answering these critical questions brings clarity to the sponsor's expectations and thus to the workshop design.

- **What are the objectives of the training?** Use the guideline ABCD to prepare objectives: identify the Audience, describe the Behavior (what will they be able to do that they can't do now), describe the Condition (what are the circumstances under which they need to be able to do the task, for example, will they have a job aid), and then specify to what Degree (level of quality).

- **Why does the sponsor want this right now?** Is something going on in the organization of which you should be aware?
- **What is the budget?** How much time and money will be invested in the training?

Key Points

- Needs analysis identifies the gap between what the organization needs and what the employees are able to do and then determines how best to bridge that gap.
- Methods of data gathering for needs analysis include strategic needs analysis, structured interviews, surveys, focus groups, and others.
- Sometimes, needs analysis is not an option, but some minimum information is necessary, including who wants the training, how the results will be defined, why the training is being requested now, and what the budget is.

What to Do Next

- If you have the option, carry out a needs analysis to determine if this training is really what your organization requires to succeed. If it isn't, prepare to argue against wasting time, money, and effort on training that will not support the organization's goals.
- If you don't have the option of a needs analysis, make sure that you seek out at least the bare minimum information to conduct effective training.
- Prepare the learning objectives using ABCD (identifying audience, behavior, condition, and degree).
- If you have little training background, read the next chapter (chapter 6) to learn about the theories and concepts that are at the root of training design. If you are an experienced trainer, skim chapter 6 on design theory or go straight to chapter 8 for tips on delivering training.

Additional Resources

Biech, E., ed. (2014). *ASTD Handbook: The Definitive Reference for Training & Development*. Alexandria, VA: ASTD Press.

Biech, E., ed. (2008). *ASTD Handbook for Workplace Learning Professionals*. Alexandria, VA: ASTD Press.

Russo, C. "Be a Better Needs Analyst." ASTD Infoline no. 258502. Alexandria, VA: ASTD Press.

Tobey, D. (2005). *Needs Assessment Basics*. Alexandria, VA: ASTD Press.

Chapter 6

Understanding the Foundations of Training Design

What's in This Chapter

- Introducing adult learning theory
- Exploring multiple intelligences
- Incorporating whole brain learning
- Learning how theory enters into practice

Because this book provides a fully designed workshop, you don't need to know all the details of designing a course—the design has already been done for you. However, understanding some of the principle design and learning theories that underpin this workshop is useful and helpful—especially if you are somewhat new to the field of workplace training and development. To effectively deliver training to learners requires a core understanding of how and why people learn. This gives you the flexibility to adapt a course to the unique learners in the room as needed.

When designing a communication skills workshop, paying attention to content flow is especially important. While there is no one right way to flow communication skills content, you must ensure that the topics build on one another and that you solidly connect the concepts and ideas together so you leverage the most of the learning opportunity. Great communication skills require practice, so always include interactive practice sessions in the design of the workshop. Short but well-designed activities can have significant impact.

Basic Adult Learning Theory

The individual trainee addressed in these workshops is typically an adult with learning needs that differ in many (but not all) ways from children. Much has been documented about how adults learn best. A key figure in adult education is Malcolm Knowles, who is often regarded as the father of adult learning. Knowles made several contributions to the field but is best known for popularizing the term *andragogy*, which refers to the art and science of teaching adults. Here are six assumptions about adult learners noted in *The Adult Learner: A Neglected Species* (1984):

- Adults need to know why learning something is important before they learn it.
- Adults have a concept of self and do not like others imposing their will on them.
- Adults have a wealth of knowledge and experience and want that knowledge to be recognized.
- Adults open up to learning when they think that the learning will help them with real problems.
- Adults want to know how the learning will help them in their personal lives.
- Adults respond to external motivations, such as the prospect of a promotion or an increase in salary.

Given these principles of adult learning, designing sessions that are highly interactive and engaging is critical (see sidebar on page 79 for more tips). Forcing anyone to learn anything is impossible, so the goal of effective training design is to provide every opportunity and encouragement to the potential learner. Involvement of the learner is the key. As an old Chinese proverb says, "Tell me and I will forget. Show me and I may remember. Involve me and I will understand." The designs in this book use several methods to convey information and engage participants. By incorporating varied training media—such as presentation media, discussion sessions, small-group work, structured exercises, and self-assessments—these designs maximize active participant involvement and offer something for every learning style.

In addition to engaging the interest of the learner, interactive training allows you to tap into another source of learning content: the participants themselves. In a group-learning situation, a good learning environment encourages participants to share with others in the group so the entire group's cumulative knowledge can be used.

Tips for Adult Learning

To reach adult learners, incorporate these ideas into your next training session:

- Incorporate self-directed learning activities in the session design.
- Avoid overuse of lectures and "talking to." Emphasize discussion.
- Use interactive methods such as case studies, role playing, and so forth.
- Make the content and materials closely fit assessed needs.
- Allow plenty of time to "process" the learning activities.
- Include applications planning in each learning activity.
- Promote inquiry into problems and affirm the experience of participants.
- Give participants a rationale for becoming involved and provide opportunities for success.
- Promote getting acquainted and interpersonal linkages.
- Diagnose and prioritize learning needs and preferences before and during the session.
- Use learning groups as "home bases" for participants.
- Include interpersonal feedback exercises and opportunities to experiment.
- Use subgroups to provide safety and readiness to engage in open interchange.
- Make all learner assessment self-directed.
- Provide activities that focus on cognitive, affective, and behavioral change.

Designing for Accessibility

Talent development professionals are not new to assessing needs in learning and development, however our industry has traditionally focused on topical or competency focused needs and designing relevant content that engages the learners. Designing with accessibility in mind adds another layer of complexity to our needs assessment and instructional design considerations.

Four main access needs cover most disability considerations—auditory, visual, physical, and cognitive and psychological. Many instructional design strategies accommodate more than one access need. For example, while auditory access—such as closed captioning and written video scripts—is necessary for someone who is deaf or hard of hearing, it is also beneficial for those who have learning disabilities with an auditory processing component. Similarly, visual accommodations—such as audio descriptions or auditory text to voice resources—are beneficial not only to someone who is blind or has limited vision, but also those with learning disabilities that have a visual processing component (such as dyslexia).

As you design the content for your programs, it is crucial to incorporate inclusive design strategies.

Theory Into Practice

These theories (and more that are not addressed here) affect the way the content of the workshop is put together. Some examples of training features that derive from these theories include handouts, research references, and presentation media to read; quiet time to write notes and reflect; opportunities for listening and talking; and exercises for practicing skills. The workshop activities and materials for the programs in this book have taken these theories to heart in their design, providing content, activities, and tools that will appeal to and engage many learning and thinking styles. Additional ways to translate learning and design theory into practice include the following.

Establishing a Framework

For learners to understand the goals of training and how material relates to real work situations, a framework can be helpful. When presenting the training in the context of a framework, trainers should provide an overview of why the organization has decided to undertake the training and why it is important. This explanation should also highlight what the trainer hopes to accomplish and how the skills learned in this training will be useful back on the job.

Objectives and goals of the programs and learning activities are described in this workbook; share those objectives with the learners when discussing the purposes of specific exercises. Handouts will also help provide a framework for participants.

Identifying Behaviors

Within any training goal are many behaviors. For example, listening and giving clear directions are necessary behaviors for good customer service. Customer service does not improve simply because employees are told to do so—participants need to understand the reasons and see the relevant parts of the equation. For these reasons, facilitators should identify and discuss relevant behaviors throughout the program.

Training helps people identify the behaviors that are important, so that those behaviors can be targeted for improvement. Learning activities enable participants to analyze different skills and behaviors and to separate the parts from the whole. The learning activities in this book, with their clearly stated objectives, have been carefully crafted to take these considerations into account.

Practicing

Practice is crucial for learning because learning takes place by doing and by seeing. In the training designs included in this workbook, practice occurs in written exercises, verbal exercises, and role playing. Role playing helps participants actually practice the behaviors that are being addressed. Role-play exercises bring skills and behaviors to life for those acting out particular roles and for those observing the scenarios.

Learning a new skill takes a lot of practice. Some participants learn skills more quickly than others. Some people's attitudes might prevent them from being open to trying new behaviors. Your job is to facilitate the session to the best of your ability, taking different learning styles into account. The rest is up to the participants.

Providing Feedback

A key aspect of training is the feedback trainers give to participants. If delivered in a supportive and constructive manner, feedback helps learners develop a deeper understanding of the content you are presenting and the behaviors they are practicing. Feedback in role plays is especially powerful because this is where "the rubber hits the road." In role plays, observers can see if people are able to practice the behaviors that have been discussed, or whether habitual responses will prevail.

Making It Relevant

Throughout the program you will discuss how to use skills and new behaviors on the job. These discussions will help answer the question "So what?" Exercises and action plans help participants bring new skills back to actual work situations. This is also important in addressing the adult need for relevancy in learning.

The Bare Minimum

- **Model it.** Communication is one of those unique topics that require designers to practice what they preach. All correspondence and communications with the participants should be well written and free of typographical errors. Supplemental workshop materials such as slides, handouts, and activities should be clear, concise, complete, correct, and considerate—demonstrating the Five Cs of Effective Communication.

- **Keep the focus on self-reflection.** Be purposeful in designing content that encourages participants to analyze their own behaviors instead of what others do wrong.
- **Build practice into the design.** As with many skills, communication improves with practice. Provide your participants with hands-on, engaging opportunities to practice the correct skills.

Key Points

- Adults have specific learning needs that must be addressed in training to make it successful.
- People also have different intelligences; that is, different areas in which they are more comfortable and competent. Addressing different intelligences in the workshop keeps more people engaged in more ways.
- People take in new information in different ways; so addressing a variety of different thinking styles can help everyone learn more effectively.
- Some important ways of bringing theory into practice are creating a framework, identifying behaviors, practicing, providing feedback, and making the learning relevant.

What to Do Next

- Look through the training materials to identify how they address the learning theories presented in this book. If you make modifications to the material, consider whether those modifications leave out an intelligence or a thinking style. Can you address more intelligences without making the material cumbersome?
- Read the next chapter to learn ways you can improve your facilitation skills. Many of these skills will also be useful when using learning technologies, especially collaboration tools.

Additional Resources

Biech, E., ed. (2008). *ASTD Handbook for Workplace Learning Professionals*. Alexandria, VA: ASTD Press.

Biech, E., ed. (2014). *ASTD Handbook: The Definitive Reference for Training & Development,* 2nd edition. Alexandria, VA: ASTD Press.

Gardner, H. (2006). *Multiple Intelligences: New Horizons in Theory and Practice*. New York: Basic Books.

Gardner, H. (2011). *Frames of Mind: The Theory of Multiple Intelligences*. New York: Basic Books.

Herrmann, N. (1988). *Creative Brain*. Lake Lure, NC: Brain Books.

Herrmann, N. (1996). *Whole Brain Business Book*. San Francisco: McGraw-Hill.

Herrmann-Nehdi, A. (2008). "The Learner: What We Need to Know." In E. Biech, ed., *ASTD Handbook for Workplace Learning Professionals*, 2nd edition. Alexandria, VA: ASTD Press.

Jones, J.E., W.L. Bearley, and D.C. Watsabaugh. (1996). *The New Fieldbook for Trainers: Tips, Tools, and Techniques.* Amherst, MA: HRD Press.

Knowles, M.S. (1984). *The Adult Learner: A Neglected Species.* Houston, TX: Gulf Publishing.

Russell, L. (1999). *The Accelerated Learning Fieldbook: Making the Instructional Process Fast, Flexible, and Fun.* San Francisco: Jossey-Bass/Pfeiffer.

Chapter 7

Delivering Your Communication Skills Workshop: Be a Great Facilitator

What's in This Chapter

- Defining the facilitator's role
- Creating an effective learning environment
- Preparing participant materials
- Using program preparation checklists
- Starting and ending on a strong note
- Managing participant behaviors

Let's get one thing clear from the get-go: Facilitating a workshop—facilitating learning—is *not* lecturing. The title of ATD's bestselling book says it all: *Telling Ain't Training* (Stolovitch and Keeps 2011). A facilitator is the person who helps learners open themselves to new learning and makes the process easier. The role requires that you avoid projecting yourself as a subject matter expert (SME) and that you prepare activities that foster learning through "hands-on" experience and interaction.

Before you can help someone else learn, you must understand the roles you will embody when you deliver training: trainer, facilitator, and learner. When a workshop begins, you are the trainer, bringing to the learning event a plan, structure, experience, and objectives. This is only possible because you have a strong, repeatable logistics process. As you ask the learners to prioritize the learning objectives, you slowly release control, inviting them to become partners in their own learning. As you move from the trainer role into the facilitator role, the objectives are the contract between the learners and the facilitator. All great facilitators also have a third role in the classroom—the role of learner. If you are open, you can learn many new things when you are in class. If you believe you must be the expert as a learning facilitator, you will not be very effective.

To be most successful as a learning facilitator, consider this checklist:

- ☐ Identify the beliefs that limit your ability to learn and, therefore, to teach.
- ☐ Learning is a gift for you and from you to others.
- ☐ Choose carefully what you call yourself and what you call your outcomes.
- ☐ Clarify your purpose to better honor your roles at a learning event.
- ☐ If you can't teach with passion, don't do it.

This last point is especially important. Not everyone is destined to be a great facilitator and teacher, but you can still have enormous impact if you are passionate about the topic, the process, and about helping people improve their working lives. If you are serious about becoming a great facilitator, chapter 11 provides a comprehensive assessment instrument to help you manage your personal development and increase the effectiveness of your communication skills training (see Assessment 4). You can use this instrument for self-assessment, end-of-course feedback, observer feedback, or as a professional growth tracker.

With these points firmly in mind—facilitating is not lecturing and passion can get you past many facilitator deficiencies—let's look at some other important aspects of facilitating, starting with how to create an engaging and effective learning environment.

The Learning Environment

Colors, tools, environmental considerations (such as your web background if presenting using video), and your attitude, dress, preparation, and passion all enhance—or detract from—an effective and positive learning environment. This section describes some ways to maximize learning through environmental factors.

A Note From the Author

You don't need to be a subject matter expert to facilitate a course on communication skills, but your audience does expect you to be a good communicator. Be sure to model effective written and oral communication with all pre-workshop communication messages. There are few things worse than typographical or grammatical errors in promotional messages or participant materials for a workshop espousing effective communication skills.

In addition, you should fully understand each activity so that you are comfortable facilitating it. Communication skills workshops are more engaging when facilitators share relevant (and sometimes personal) stories about a skill that they are teaching; storytelling in training helps solidify the learning.

Color. Research has shown that bland, neutral environments are so unlike the real world that learning achieved in these "sensory deprivation chambers" cannot be transferred to the job. Color can be a powerful way to engage the limbic part of the brain and create long-term retention. It can align the right and left brains. Ways to incorporate color include artwork, plants, and pictures in the online environment that help people feel comfortable and visually stimulated. Consider designing and distributing color versions of your handouts and assessments. The training support materials provided in this book are designed in color but can be printed either color or in grayscale (to reduce reproduction costs).

Room Setup. You will likely be delivering your training with your webcam on. Please take some time to test your webcam. Check your background, and make sure there is nothing distracting that will detract from your message. If you plan on having attendees use their webcams, encourage them to do the same.

Your Secret Weapon. Finally, the key to establishing the optimal learning environment is *you*. You set the tone by your attitude, the way you greet people, the clothes you wear, your passion, and your interest and care for the participants. You set the stage for learning with four conditions that only you as the facilitator can create to maximize learning:

1. **Confidentiality.** Establish the expectation that anything shared during the training program will remain confidential among participants and that as the facilitator you are committed to creating a safe environment. An important step in learning is first admitting ignorance, which has some inherent risk. Adult learners may resist admitting their learning needs because they fear the repercussions of showing their weaknesses. You

can alleviate these concerns by assuring participants that the sole purpose of the training is to build their skills. Your workshop must be a safe place to learn and take risks.

2. **Freedom from distractions.** One of the single biggest challenges of virtual training is having the learners' full attention and keeping them from multitasking. Ahead of your first session, encourage attendees to fully block their calendars and move any meetings or calls.

   a. Ask that attendees close any other applications, including email for the duration of the training.

   b. Acknowledge that participants probably feel they shouldn't be away from work; remind them that the purpose of the training is to improve their work lives.

   c. Ask that cell phone notifications be turned off or set to silent alerts.

   d. Emphasize that because they are spending this time in training, trainees should immerse themselves in the learning experience and thereby maximize the value of their time away from work responsibilities.

3. **Personal responsibility for learning.** A facilitator can only create the *opportunity* for learning. Experiential learning requires that participants actively engage with and commit to learning—they cannot sit back and soak up information like sponges.

4. **Group participation.** Each participant brings relevant knowledge to the training program. Through discussion and sharing of information, a successful training session will tap into the knowledge of each participant. Encourage all participants to accept responsibility for helping others learn.

Program Preparation Checklist

Preparation is power when it comes to facilitating a successful workshop, and a checklist is a powerful tool for effective preparation. This checklist of activities will help you prepare your workshop:

☐ Write down all login and tech requirement details when scheduling the workshop.

☐ Send a contract to the client to confirm details, or if you are an internal facilitator, develop guidelines and a workshop structure in conjunction with appropriate supervisors and managers.

☐ Specify platform and hardware requirements details in writing and then confirm with the organization that participants will have access to these.

- [ ] Define goals and expectations for the workshop.

- [ ] Get a list of participants, titles, roles, and responsibilities.

- [ ] Send participants a questionnaire that requires them to confirm their goals for the workshop.

- [ ] Send the client (or the participants, if you are an internal facilitator) an agenda for the workshop, with times for breaks and meals.

- [ ] Create polls, breakout rooms, and other interactive features if it's possible to do so in advance on the platform you'll be using.

- [ ] Confirm whether you or your internal/external client will distribute electronic copies of the workshop handouts. The workshop handouts should include all tools, training instruments, assessments, and worksheets. You may choose also to include copies of the PowerPoint slides as part of the participant guide. All the supplemental materials you need to conduct the workshops in this book are available for download (see chapter 13 for instructions).

- [ ] Find out if participants would like to receive pre-reading materials electronically before the session.

- [ ] Prepare assessments, tools, training instruments, and workshop materials at least one week before the workshop so that you have time to peruse and check them and assemble any equipment you may need (see the next two sections).

Participant Materials

Participant materials support participant learning throughout the workshop and provide continuing references after the workshop has ended. There are several kinds of participant materials. Here are some options:

Handouts

The development and "look" of your handouts are vital to help participants understand the information they convey. To compile the handouts properly, first gather all assessments, tools, training instruments, activities, and PowerPoint slides and arrange them in the order they appear in the workshop. Then if you are planning on mailing physical copies to participants, bind them together in some fashion. There are several options for compiling your material, ranging from inexpensive to deluxe. The kind of binding is your choice—materials can be stapled, spiral bound, or gathered in a ring binder—but remember that a professional look supports success. Your choice of binding will depend on your budget for the project. Because first appearances count, provide a cover with eye-catching colors and appropriate graphics.

Using the agendas in chapters 1–3, select the presentation slides, learning activities, handouts, tools, and assessments appropriate to your workshop (see chapter 13: Online Tools and Downloads). If you choose to print out the presentation slides for your participants, consider printing no more than three slides per handout page to keep your content simple with sufficient white space for the participants to write their own notes. Use the learning objectives for each workshop to provide clarity for the participants at the outset. Remember to number the pages, to add graphics for interest (and humor), and to include bookmarks for easy reference if the materials have multiple sections.

Some participants like to receive the handouts before the workshop begins. You may want to email participants to determine when and how they would like to receive the handouts.

Presentation Slides

This ATD Workshop Series book includes presentation slides to support the two-day, one-day, and half-day agendas. They have been crafted to adhere to presentation best practices. If you choose to reorder or otherwise modify the slides, keep in mind these important concepts.

When you use PowerPoint software as a teaching tool, be judicious in the number of slides that you prepare. In a scientific lecture, slides are usually a necessity for explaining formulas or results, but a communication workshop relies on interaction so keep the slide information simple. Also, do not include more than five or six bullet points per slide. See more tips for effective PowerPoint slides in Figure 7-1.

A message can be conveyed quickly through the use of simple graphics. For example, an illustration of two people in conversation may highlight interpersonal communication; a photo of a boardroom-style meeting may illustrate a group engaged in negotiation.

When you use presentation slides ask yourself: What will a slide add to my presentation? Ensure that the answer that comes back is "it will enhance the message." If slides are simply used to make the workshop look more sophisticated or technical, the process may not achieve the desired results.

It can be frustrating when a facilitator shows a slide for every page that the participants have in front of them. The dynamics of the class are likely to disconnect. If the information you are teaching is in the handouts or workbook, work from those media alone and keep the workshop personally interactive.

Figure 7-1. Tips for Effective PowerPoint Slides

Slides can enhance your presentation. They can also detract from it by being too cluttered, monotonous, or hard to read. Here are some tips for clear, effective slides:

Fonts

- Use sans-serif fonts such as Arial, Calibri, or Helvetica; these are more easily read on LCD screens and in video/web presentations.
- Use the same sans-serif font for most (if not all) of the presentation.
- Use a font size no smaller than 24 points. (This will also help keep the number of bullets per slide down.)
- Consider using a 32-point font—this is the easiest for web/video transmission.
- Limit yourself to one font size per slide.

Colors

- Font colors should be black or dark blue for light backgrounds and white or yellow on dark backgrounds. Think high contrast for clarity and visual impact.
- Avoid using red or green. It doesn't transfer well when used in a webinar and causes issues for people who suffer color blindness.

Text and Paragraphs

- Align text left or right, not centered.
- Avoid cluttering a slide—use a single headline and a few bullet points.
- Use no more than six words to a line; avoid long sentences.
- Use sentence case—ALL CAPS ARE DIFFICULT TO READ AND CAN FEEL LIKE YELLING.
- Avoid abbreviations and acronyms.
- Limit use of punctuation marks.

Source: Cat Russo (2014).

Workbooks and Journals

A participant journal can be included with your handouts, or it may be a separate entity. Throughout the workshop participants can assess their progress and advance their development by entering details of their personal learning in the journal. The benefit of this journal to participants is that they can separate their personal discoveries and development from the main workshop handouts and use this journal as an action plan if desired.

Videos

If you show a video in your workshop, ensure that the skills it contains are up to date and that the video is less than 20 minutes long. Provide questions that will lead to a discussion of the information viewed. Short video clips can be effective learning tools.

A Strong Start: Introduction, Icebreakers, and Openers

The start of a session is a crucial time in the workshop dynamic. How the participants respond to you, the facilitator, can set the mood for the remainder of the workshop. To get things off on the right foot, log in to the training room early, at least 30 to 60 minutes before the workshop. This gives you time not only to set up slides and breakout rooms if that has not already been done, but also to test the environment, the equipment, and your place in the room. When participants begin to arrive (and some of them come very early), be ready to welcome them. Don't be distracted with problems or issues; be free and available to them.

While they are settling in, engage them with simple questions:

- Where are you calling in from?
- What was the last movie you saw?
- May I help you with anything?

When the participants have arrived and settled, introduce yourself. Write a humorous introduction, if that's your style, because this will help you be more approachable. Talk more about what you want to accomplish in the workshop than about your accomplishments. If you have a short biographical piece included in the handouts or in the workbook, it may serve as your personal introduction.

At the conclusion of your introduction, provide an activity in which participants can meet each other (often called an icebreaker). Because participants sometimes come into a training session feeling inexperienced, skeptical, reluctant, or scared, using icebreaker activities to open training enables participants to interact in a fun and nonthreatening way and to warm up the group before approaching more serious content. Don't limit the time on this too much unless you have an extremely tight schedule. The more time participants spend getting to know each other at the beginning of the workshop, the more all of you will benefit as the session proceeds.

Feedback

Feedback is the quickest, surest way for you, the facilitator, to learn if the messages and instruction are reaching the participants and if the participants are absorbing the content. It is also important for you to evaluate the participants' rate of progress and learning. Answers to the questions you ask throughout the workshop will help you identify much of the progress, but these answers come from only a few of the participants at a time. They're not a global snapshot of the entire group's comprehension and skills mastery.

When you lead a workshop, the participants walk a fine line between retention and deflection of knowledge. Continuing evaluations ensure that learning is taking root. Three levels of questions—learning comprehension, skills mastery, and skills application—help you determine where the training may not be achieving the intended results.

- Learning comprehension checks that the participants understand and grasp the skills being taught (see Figure 7-2).

- Skills mastery means that the participants are able to demonstrate their newly acquired knowledge by some activity, such as teaching a portion of a module to their fellow participants or delivering their interpretation of topic specifics to the class (see Figure 7-3). See also Assessment 10: Skills Mastery Assessment for an instrument to help your participants address this issue.

- Skills application is the real test. You may choose to substantiate this through role plays or group case studies. When the participants have the opportunity to verbally communicate the skills learned and to reach desired results through such application, then skills application is established (see Figure 7-4). See also Assessment 9: Skills Application Reflection for an instrument to help your participants identify ways to apply the skills they've learned back in the workplace.

The questions in Figures 7-2 to 7-4 are designed for written answers so you can incorporate them into the takeaway workbook you create. (See Assessments 9 and 10.) The questions concerning skills mastery and skills application could be set as homework if the workshop is longer than one day. Keep in mind that you will also reevaluate after each day of a multiday session.

Figure 7-2. Learning Comprehension Questions

Here are some questions that can be asked to determine each participant's level of *learning comprehension*:

- Give a brief overview of your learning in this workshop. (Begin your phrases with "I have learned. . . ." This will assist you in focusing your responses.)
- How/where will you apply this knowledge in your workplace?
- Did you acquire this knowledge through lectures, practice, discussion, or a combination of all methods?
- Do you feel sufficiently confident to pass on this knowledge to your colleagues?
- Are there any areas that will require additional learning for you to feel sufficiently confident?

Figure 7-3. Skills Mastery Questions

Now let's look at some questions you can use to evaluate your trainees' *skills mastery*:

- If you were asked to teach one skill in this workshop, which skill would it be?
- What would your three key message points be for that skill?
- Describe the steps you would take to instruct each message point (for example, lecture, group discussion, or PowerPoint presentation).
- What methods would you use to ensure that your participants comprehend your instruction?
- Would feedback from your participants, both positive and negative, affect the development of your skills mastery? If yes, illustrate your response and the changes you would make.

Figure 7-4. Skills Application Questions

And finally, let's consider some questions that identify participants' *ability to apply the skills* they've learned in the workshop:

- Please describe a situation at your workplace where you could employ one specific communication skill from this workshop.
- How would you introduce this skill to your colleagues?
- How would you set goals to measure the improvement in this skill?
- Describe the input and participation you would expect from your colleagues.
- How would you exemplify mastery of the skill?

Let's now look at other forms of in-class learning assessments: role plays, participant presentations, and journaling.

Role Plays

Role plays are an effective tool for assessing learning comprehension. If two or more participants conduct a role play that reveals their understanding of the information, with an outcome that reflects that understanding, then it becomes a "live feed," instantaneous learning for all.

You must set up the role play carefully. It is often wise for you to be a part of the first role-play experience to show participants how it's done and to make them more comfortable with the activity. Ensure that you explain all the steps of the role play and the desired outcome. It is insightful to role play a negative version first, followed by participant discussion; then role play a positive aspect the second time. For example, if confrontational communication is the topic and the situation under discussion involves a line manager and his or her supervisor, first enact the role play using the verbal and body language that is causing the negative result. Discuss this as a class to identify the specific language that needs improvement. Then enact the role play again, this time using positive language.

Frequently it is helpful for a participant who has been on the receiving end of negative communication in their workplace to adopt the role of deliverer. Walking in the other person's shoes leads to a quicker understanding of the transaction. This positive role play should also be followed by whole-group discussion of the elements that worked. Participants can be invited to write about the process and its results to give them a real-life example to take back to the workplace.

Participant Presentations

You might ask a participant to present a module of learning to the workshop. This allows the facilitator to observe the participants from a different perspective—both as listeners and as presenters. Be ready to assist or to answer questions. For example, a participant may choose assertive communication as their module, and the specific issue on return to the workplace may be a request for promotion. The participant defines and delivers the steps required to ask for the promotion while the facilitator and other participants observe and evaluate the success of the approach and demonstration of confidence and assertiveness.

Journaling

Keeping a journal is a quiet, introspective way for participants to get a grip on their learning. When you complete an activity, have everyone take five minutes to write a summary of the skill just learned and then ask them to share what they've written with a partner. Invite the partner to correct and improve the material if necessary or appropriate.

Questioning Skills

When participants are asking questions, they are engaged and interested. Your responses to questions will augment the learning atmosphere. The way in which you respond is extremely important. Answers that are evasive can disturb a class because they cast doubts on your credibility. Glib or curt answers are insulting. Lengthy responses break the rhythm of the class and often go off track. When dealing with questions, the value of effective communication is in hearing the question, answering the question asked, and moving on. Repeat questions so that all participants hear them. In addition, this can ensure that you have heard the question correctly.

However, don't rush to answer. Take time to let everyone absorb the information. When time is of the essence, don't be tempted to give long, complicated answers that embrace additional topics. Be courteous and clear. Check that your answer has been understood. When a question comes up that could possibly derail the session or that is beyond the scope of the topic, you can choose to record it on a "parking lot" list and then revisit it later at an assigned time. A parking lot can be as simple as a list on a whiteboard. However, whenever possible, answer a question at the time it is asked. Consider answering with analogies when they are appropriate because these often help elucidate challenging concepts.

Effective questions that prompt answers are open ended:

- What have you learned so far?
- How do you feel about this concept?
- How would you handle this situation?

Any question that begins with "what" or "how" promotes a more extensive answer. Questions that begin with "why"—as in "why do you think that way?"—can promote defensiveness.

When a participant asks a confrontational or negative question, handle it with dignity and do not become aggressive. It's helpful to ask open-ended questions of the participant to try to clarify the original question. For example, ask, "What do you mean by . . . ?" or "Which part of the activity do you find challenging?" This form of open-ended questioning requires additional accountability from the participant. The reason for the confrontation may have arisen from confusion about the information or the need to hear their own thoughts aloud. When you are calm and patient, the altercation is more likely to be resolved. If the participant persists, you may wish to ask them to discuss the specifics in a private setting. More ideas for dealing with difficult participants are provided later in this chapter.

Some participants enjoy being questioned because it gives them an opportunity to show their knowledge. Others are reticent for fear of looking foolish if they don't know the answer. Because your trainees have unique styles and personalities, always have a purpose for asking questions: Will these questions test the participants' knowledge? Are these questions appropriate? Are you asking them in the style that suits the participant?

Training Platform and Participant Management

When everything is in place and ready for the session, it's time to review the "soft skills" portion of your responsibilities—that is, how you conduct the workshop and interact with participants. Here are some things to consider:

- **"Respect and respond" should be a facilitator's mantra.** At all times respect the participants and respond in a timely manner.

- **Manage workshop program time.** This is vital because it ensures that the goals will be met in the time allotted.

- **Read the participants' body language if they're using video.** This will help you know when to pause and ask questions or to give them a stretch break.

- **Answer questions fully and effectively.** If you don't know an answer, open the question up to the participants or offer to get back to the questioner. Make a note to remind yourself to do so.

- **Add a "parking lot"**—a whiteboard or other feature where content can be created and posted for future reference. When questions arise that are out of step with the current communication activity, ask the participant to write the question in the parking lot. When the current activity is completed, you can address the questions parked there.

- **Control unruly participants through assertiveness of vocal tone and message.** When appropriate, invite them to help you with tasks because frequently they just need to be more involved.

- **Be sure to monitor a participant who is slower to assimilate the information.** If time permits, give that trainee some one-on-one time with you.

- **Keep your energy high.** Inject humor wherever possible. Ensure the learning is taking root.

A Word About Dealing With Difficult Participants

Much of the preparation you do before a training session will help you minimize disruptive behavior in your training session. But, sadly, you are still likely at some point to have difficult participants in your training room. Beyond preparation, you may need some specific strategies to help you manage disruptions and keep the learning on track. Figure 7-5, drawn from McCain and Tobey's *Facilitation Basics* (2004), identifies many of these behaviors and gives strategies for nipping them in the bud.

Figure 7-5. Managing Difficult Participants

THE PROBLEM	THE SOLUTION
Carrying on a Side Conversation	• Don't assume the talkers are being disrespectful; depersonalize the behavior by thinking: "Maybe they are unclear about a point in the material, or the material is not relevant to their needs." • Ask the talkers if they don't understand something.
Monopolizing the Discussion	• Some participants tend to take over the conversation; while the enthusiasm is great, you don't want to leave other learners out. • Tell the monopolizer that their comments are valuable and interesting, but you would like to open up the discussion to others in the group. Then call on another person by name. • Enlist the monopolizer to help you by being a gatekeeper and ensuring that no one monopolizes the conversation.
Complaining	• Don't assume someone who complains doesn't have a valid reason to do so. • Ask the rest of the group if they feel the same way. If they do, try to address the issue as appropriate. • If they don't, talk to the individual separately during the break.
Challenging Your Knowledge	• Determine if this person really knows more than you do, or is just trying to act as though they do. • If they do know more, try to enlist their help in the training. • If they don't, ask them to provide expertise and they will usually realize they can't and back down.
Daydreaming	• Use the person's name in an example to get her attention. • Switch to something more active. • If behavior affects more than just one person, try to find out if something work-related is causing it and have a brief discussion about it.
Heckling	• Don't get upset or start volleying remarks. • Try giving the person learning-oriented attention: "John, you clearly have some background in this area; would you care to share your thoughts with the rest of the group?" • Get the attention off you by switching to a group-oriented activity.
Clowning Around	• Give the person attention in a learning-oriented way by calling on them to answer a question or be a team leader. • If a joke is intended to relieve tension in the session and others seem to be experiencing it, deal with the tension head on by bringing it up. • If it is just a joke, and it's funny and appropriate, laugh!

THE PROBLEM	THE SOLUTION
Making an Insensitive Remark	• Remember that if the person truly didn't intend offense, you don't want to humiliate them. But you do need to ensure that the person and everyone else in the room know that you will not tolerate bigoted or otherwise inappropriate remarks. • Give the person a chance to retract what they said by asking if that is what they meant to say. If it wasn't, then move on. • If it was, you need to let the person know that the comment is not in line with the values of your organization and it can't be allowed to continue. • If the person persists, speak to them separately, or as a last resort, ask them to leave.
Doing Other Work	• Talk to the person at a break to find out if the workshop is meeting their needs. • If the person is truly under too much pressure, offer to have them come to another session.
Not Talking	• If you can tell the person is engaged because they are taking notes, maintaining eye contact, or leaning forward, you can leave them alone. • Give the person opportunities to interact at a greater comfort level by participating in small groups or in pairs.
Withdrawing	• Talk to the person at break to find out if something is going on. Deal with the issue as appropriate. • If the person feels excluded, have them act as a team leader for a turn, or ensure that all members of teams are given opportunities to participate.
Missing the Point	• If someone misses the point, be sensitive in dealing with them. Try to find something to agree with in their point. • Try to identify what the person is having trouble grasping and clear up the point with an analogy or an example. • Never laugh at the person or otherwise humiliate them.

Source: McCain and Tobey (2004).

When all else fails, you have a few last resorts, although you would clearly rather not get to that point. One option is to simply pull aside the individual who is disrupting the class and talk to them privately. Dick Grote suggests in "Dealing with Miscreants, Snivelers, and Adversaries" that you can often catch someone off guard by asking: "Is it personal?" The direct question will usually cause the individual to deny that it is personal. Next, you tell the person that the behavior is unacceptable and that you will speak to a supervisor or training sponsor if it continues. This often works.

However, if it does not work, you can ask to have the person removed or cancel the program and speak to the person's supervisor. Clearly, these are not options to be taken lightly, but realize that they are available when you are faced with truly recalcitrant behavior.

Follow up when you have faced a difficult situation. Take some time to reflect on the event and write down the details of what happened. If possible, get perspectives and feedback from participants who witnessed it. If outside perspectives are not an option, think about the event from the points of view of the disruptive individual and other participants and ask yourself: What went wrong? What went well? How could I manage the situation better next time?

An Unforgettable End

In Biech (2008, 315), contributor Mel Silberman explains that:

> Many training programs run out of steam in the end. In some cases, participants are marking time until the close is near. In other cases, facilitators are valiantly trying to cover what they haven't got to before time runs out. How unfortunate! What happens at the end needs to be "unforgettable." You want participants to remember what they've learned. You also want participants to think what they've learned has been special.

Silberman suggests considering four areas when preparing to end your workshop:

- How will participants review what you've taught them?
- How will participants assess what they have learned?
- What will participants do about what they have learned?
- How will participants celebrate their accomplishments?

For example, consider what you've learned in this chapter. You've developed a well-rounded picture of what it takes to create an optimal, effective learning environment, from creating an inviting and engaging space to preparing and gathering materials that will make you feel like an organizational champ. You're ready to get the training off to a productive start, to manage difficult participants and situations, and to pull it all together in a powerful way. Now jump down to the end of the chapter to determine what the next steps are and take pride in the preparation that will enable you to adapt and thrive in the training room.

The Bare Minimum

- **Keep things moving.** Create an engaging, interactive environment.

- **Pay attention to the energy in the room.** Be prepared to adjust the activities as needed. Build in content that can be delivered standing or through networking activities to get participants out of their seats when needed.

- **Have fun!** If you create an upbeat tone and enjoy yourself, the participants are likely to have fun as well.

Key Points

- Facilitation is not lecturing. It's providing learning activities and support to make learning easier for the participant.

- Facilitation is not about the facilitator—it's about the learner.

- An inviting space and a safe, collaborative environment are necessary for learning to occur.

- Good facilitation starts with passion and significant attention to preparation.

- A good start sets the tone for the whole training session.

- A strong ending helps learners to remember the training and carry lessons forward into their work.

What to Do Next

- Prepare, modify, and review the training agenda. Use one of the agendas in section I as a starting point.

- Review the program preparation checklist and work through it step by step.

- Make a list of required participant materials and facilitator equipment and begin assembling them.

- Review all learning activities included in the agenda and start practicing your delivery.

Additional Resources

Biech, E. (2006). *90 World-Class Activities by 90 World-Class Trainers.* San Francisco: John Wiley/Pfeiffer.

Biech, E. (2008). *10 Steps to Successful Training.* Alexandria, VA: ASTD Press.

Biech, E., ed. (2014). *ASTD Handbook: The Definitive Reference for Training & Development.* Alexandria, VA: ASTD Press.

Duarte, N. (2010). *Resonate: Present Visual Stories That Transform Audiences.* Hoboken, NJ: Wiley.

Grote, D. (1998). "Dealing with Miscreants, Snivelers, and Adversaries," *Training & Development*, 52(10), October.

McCain, D.V., and D. Tobey. (2004). *Facilitation Basics.* Alexandria, VA: ASTD Press.

Stolovitch, H.D., and E.J. Keeps. (2011). *Tellling Ain't Training,* 2nd edition. Alexandria, VA: ASTD Press.

Thiagarajan, S. (2005). *Thiagi's Interactive Lectures: Power Up Your Training With Interactive Games and Exercises.* Alexandria, VA: ASTD Press.

Thiagarajan, S. (2006). *Thiagi's 100 Favorite Games.* San Francisco: John Wiley/Pfeiffer.

Chapter 8

Evaluating Workshop Results

What's in This Chapter

- Exploring the reasons to evaluate your program
- Introducing the levels of measurement and what they measure

---

Evaluation represents the last letter of the ADDIE cycle of instructional design (analysis, design, development, implementation, and evaluation). Although evaluation is placed at the end of the model, an argument could be made for including it far earlier, as early as the design and development phase and perhaps even in the analysis phase. Why? Because the goals of the training, or the learning objectives (see chapter 5), provide insight into what the purpose of the evaluation should be. In fact, business goals, learning goals, and evaluation of those goals are useful subjects to address with organizational leaders or the training sponsor. Trainers often begin a program without thinking about how the program fits into a strategic plan or how it supports and promotes specific business goals, but these are critical to consider before implementing the program.

However, this chapter is not about that upfront evaluation of the program design and materials; it is about evaluating the program after it has been delivered and reporting the results back to the training sponsor. This form of evaluation allows you to determine whether the program objectives were achieved and whether the learning was applied on the job and had an impact on the business. Evaluation can also serve as the basis for future program and budget discussions with training sponsors.

A Note From the Author

Measuring the impact of any soft skills training can be challenging, even more so with communication skills training because so many factors can affect communication. Start early in the design process to include organizational goals as well as individual learning goals. Clarifying expectations of which specific communication skills are needed in an organization will not only improve your program design but will also help you decide what to measure and at what level to measure it.

Levels of Measurement

No discussion of measurement would be complete without an introduction to the concepts that underpin the field of evaluation. The following is a brief primer on a very large and detailed subject that can be somewhat overwhelming. If your organization is committed to measuring beyond Level 2, take some time to read the classics of evaluation.

In 1956/57, Donald Kirkpatrick, one of the leading experts in measuring training results, identified four levels of measurement and evaluation. These four levels build successively from the simplest (Level 1) to the most complex (Level 4) levels of evaluation and are based on information gathered at previous levels. For that reason, determining upfront at what level to evaluate a program is important. A general rule of thumb is that the more important or fundamental the training is and the greater the investment in it, the higher the level of evaluation to use. The four basic levels of evaluation are

- **Level 1—Reaction:** Measures how participants react to the workshop.
- **Level 2—Learning:** Measures whether participants have learned and understood the content of the workshop.
- **Level 3—Behavior (also referred to as application):** Measures on-the-job changes that have occurred because of the learning.
- **Level 4—Results:** Measures the impact of training on the bottom line.

These four levels correspond with the evaluation methods described below.

Level 1. Measuring Participant Reactions

One of the most common ways trainers use to measure participants' reactions is by administering end-of-session evaluation forms, often called "smile sheets" (for a sample, see Assessment 3:

Course Evaluation). The main benefit of using smile sheets is that they are easy to create and administer. If you choose this method, consider the suggestions below, but first decide the purpose of evaluating. Do you want to know if the participants enjoyed the presentation? How they felt about the facilities? Or how they reacted to the content?

Here are a few suggestions for creating evaluation forms:

- Keep the form to one page.
- Make your questions brief.
- Leave adequate space for comments.
- Group types of questions into categories (for example, cluster questions about content, questions about the instructor, and questions about materials).
- Provide variety in types of questions (include multiple-choice, true-false, short-answer, and open-ended items).
- Include relevant decision makers in your questionnaire design.
- Plan how you will use and analyze the data and create a design that will facilitate your analysis.
- Use positively worded items (such as, "I listen to others," instead of "I don't listen to others").

You can find additional tips for creating smile sheets and evaluating their results in "Making Smile Sheets Count" by Nancy S. Kristiansen (2004).

Although smile sheets are used frequently, they have some inherent limitations. For example, participants cannot judge the *effectiveness* of training techniques. In addition, results can be overly influenced by the personality of the facilitator or participants' feelings about having to attend training. Be cautious of relying solely on Level 1 evaluations.

Level 2. Measuring the Extent to Which Participants Have Learned

If you want to determine the extent to which participants have understood the content of your workshop, testing is an option. Comparing pre-training and post-training test results indicates the amount of knowledge gained. Or you can give a quiz that tests conceptual information 30 to 60 days after the training to see if people remember the concepts. Because most adult learners do not generally like the idea of tests, you might want to refer to these evaluations as "assessments."

Another model of testing is criterion-referenced testing (CRT), which tests the learner's performance against a given standard, such as "greets the customer and offers assistance within one minute of entering the store" or "initiates the landing gear at the proper time and altitude." Such testing can be important in determining whether a learner can carry out the task, determining the efficacy of the training materials, and providing a foundation for further levels of evaluation. Coscarelli and Shrock (2008) describe a five-step method for developing CRTs that include:

1. Determining what to test (analysis)

2. Determining if the test measures what it purports to measure (validity)

3. Writing test items

4. Establishing a cut-off or mastery score

5. Showing that the test provides consistent results (reliability)

Level 3. Measuring the Results of Training Back on the Job

The next level of evaluation identifies whether the learning was actually used back on the job. It is important to recognize that application on the job is where learning actually begins to have real-world effects and that application is not solely up to the learner. Many elements affect transfer and application, including follow-up, manager support, and so forth. For example, consider a sales training attendee who attends training and learns a new, more efficient way to identify sales leads. However, upon returning to work, the attendee's manager does not allow the time for the attendee to practice applying those new skills in the workplace. Over time, the training is forgotten, and any value it may have had does not accrue.

Methods for collecting data regarding performance back on the job include reports by people who manage participants, reports from staff and peers, observations, quality monitors, and other quality and efficiency measures. In "The Four Levels of Evaluation," Don Kirkpatrick (2007) provides some guidelines for carrying out Level 3 evaluations:

- Use a control group, if practical.
- Allow time for behavior change to take place.
- Evaluate before and after the program, if possible.
- Interview learners, their immediate managers, and possibly their subordinates and anyone else who observes their work or behavior.
- Repeat the evaluation at appropriate times.

Level 4. Measuring the Organizational Impact of Training

Level 4 identifies how learning affects business measures. Consider an example related to management training. Let's say a manager attends management training and learns several new and valuable techniques to engage employees and help keep them on track. Upon return, the manager gets support in applying the new skills and behaviors. As time passes, the learning starts to have measurable results: Retention has increased, employees are demonstrably more engaged and are producing better-quality goods, and sales increase because the quality has increased. Retention, engagement, quality, and sales are all measurable business results improved as a result of the training.

Measuring such organizational impact requires working with leaders to create and implement a plan to collect the data you need. Possible methods include customer surveys, measurements of sales, studies of customer retention or turnover, employee satisfaction surveys, and other measurements of issues pertinent to the organization.

Robert Brinkerhoff, well-known author and researcher of evaluation methods, has suggested the following method to obtain information relevant to results:

- Send out questionnaires to people who have gone through training, asking: To what extent have you used your training in a way that has made a significant business impact? (This question can elicit information that will point to business benefits and ways to use other data to measure accomplishments.)
- When you get responses back, conduct interviews to get more information.

Return on Investment

Measuring return on investment (ROI)—sometimes referred to as Level 5 evaluation—is useful and can help "sell" training to leaders. ROI measures the monetary value of business benefits such as those noted in the discussion about Level 4 and compares them with the fully loaded costs of training to provide a percentage return on training investment. Hard numbers such as these can be helpful in discussions with organizational executives about conducting further training and raise the profile of training.

ROI was popularized by Jack Phillips. More in-depth information can be found in the *ASTD Handbook of Measuring and Evaluating Training* (Phillips 2010).

Reporting Results

An important and often under-considered component of both ROI and Level 4 evaluations is reporting results. Results from these types of evaluation studies have several different audiences, and it is important to take time to plan the layout of the evaluation report and the method of delivery with the audience in question. Consider the following tasks in preparing communications:

- **Purpose:** The purposes for communicating program results depend on the specific program, the setting, and unique organizational needs.

- **Audience:** For each target audience, understand the audience and find out what information is needed and why. Take into account audience bias, and then tailor the communication to each group.

- **Timing:** Lay the groundwork for communication before program implementation. Avoid delivering a message, particularly a negative message, to an audience unprepared to hear the story and unaware of the methods that generated the results.

- **Reporting format:** The type of formal evaluation report depends on how much detailed information is presented to target audiences. Brief summaries may be sufficient for some communication efforts. In other cases, particularly programs that require significant funding, more detail may be important.

The Bare Minimum

- If formal measurement techniques are not possible, consider using the simple, interactive, informal measurement activities found in Learning Activity 24: Informal Evaluations.

- Empower the participants to create an action plan to capture the new skills and ideas they plan to use. Ultimately, the success of any training event will rest on lasting positive change in participants' behavior.

Key Points

- The four basic levels of evaluation cover reaction, learning, application, and organizational impact.

- A fifth level covers return on investment.

- Reporting results is as important as measuring them. Be strategic in crafting your results document, taking into consideration purpose, audience, timing, and format.

What to Do Next

- Identify the purpose and level of evaluation based on the learning objectives and learning goals.

- Prepare a training evaluation form, or use the one provided in chapter 11.

- If required, develop plans for follow-up evaluations to determine skills mastery, on-the-job application, and business impact.

Additional Resources

Biech, E., ed. (2014). *ASTD Handbook: The Definitive Reference for Training & Development,* 2nd edition. Alexandria, VA: ASTD Press.

Brinkerhoff, R.O. (2006). *Telling Training's Story: Evaluation Made Simple, Credible, and Effective.* San Francisco: Berrett-Koehler.

Coscarelli, W., and S. Shrock. (2008). "Level 2: Learning—Five Essential Steps for Creating Your Tests and Two Cautionary Tales." In E. Biech, ed., *ASTD Handbook for Workplace Learning Professionals.* Alexandria, VA: ASTD Press.

Kirkpatrick, D.L. (2007). "The Four Levels of Evaluation." *Infoline* No. 0701, Alexandria, VA: ASTD Press.

Kirkpatrick, D., and J.D. Kirkpatrick. (2006). *Evaluating Training Programs: The Four Levels,* 3rd edition. San Francisco: Berrett-Koehler.

Kirkpatrick, D., and J.D. Kirkpatrick. (2007). *Implementing the Four Levels: A Practical Guide for Effective Evaluation of Training Programs.* San Francisco: Berrett-Koehler.

Kristiansen, N.S. (2004). "Making Smile Sheets Count." *Infoline* No. 0402, Alexandria, VA: ASTD Press.

Phillips, P.P., ed. (2010). *ASTD Handbook of Measuring and Evaluating Training.* Alexandria, VA: ASTD Press.

SECTION III

POST-WORKSHOP LEARNING

Chapter 9

The Follow-Up Coach

What's in This Chapter

- Increasing training results through follow-up coaching
- Eight ideas for follow-up coaching
- Creating an open culture for communication

Learning to be an effective communicator is a lifelong endeavor. Attending workshops can certainly help employees communicate better; however, as with many skills, it is only with continued practice and follow-up coaching that behavior and results are refined and improved. It takes time for people to process new information, break old patterns of behavior, and start applying new skills.

Increasing Training Results Through Follow-Up: What to Do After the Workshop

The benefits of training are lost if behavioral change doesn't occur. To achieve real behavioral change, it is important that the ideas delivered in the learning environment continue to be   supported, an idea that is borne out in research on training. One study that looked at the benefits of training with and without follow-up coaching found that while training alone improved performance by 22 percent, training that included follow-up coaching improved performance by 88 percent—a dramatic increase in return on investment (Olivero, Bane, and Kopelmann 1997). It is also clear that learning is not a once-and-done event, training impact can be drastically improved through effective follow-up techniques (Martin 2010). Managers need to support behavioral change and keep the discussion alive by incorporating key communication competencies into discussions in meetings, performance expectations, individual coaching conversations, and messaging in employee communications.

One way to look at the relationship between training follow-up techniques and individual coaching is to think back to when you learned to ride a bike. First you received the initial instruction on how to ride the bike. As you practiced your new skills, you likely received additional encouragement and support, which helped you become an even stronger rider. That same formula works when helping someone become a skilled communicator. Learning to communicate effectively takes good instruction or training, repeated practice, and follow-up coaching and guidance. See the sidebar for eight ideas to help keep the learning alive.

Follow-Up Virtual Peer Interactions

In many cases, learners feel more comfortable discussing new concepts, challenges, or goals with peers as a way to bounce ideas around and find true understanding before having to present those ideas in a more charged or power-based situation, such as with a supervisor. You may consider using online collaboration tools or social media groups (such as Yammer, LinkedIn, Google+, or Facebook) to post follow-up questions or thought-provoking conversation starters to encourage participants to continue discussing key topics from the workshop. Your role here is not so much to provide input, but more to encourage participants to collaborate among themselves. Alternately, you might consider creating and scheduling small group collaboration sessions using web conferencing tools like Zoom, Google Meet, or WebEx. These sessions can be very informal (such as simple check-in type questions, what's working, what have you tried) or more structured (a facilitated discussion around a hot topic or current event) based on the needs of the group and the desired outcomes. Again, your role in these types of follow-on discussions is that of facilitator, not instructor. In either case, continued support of an ongoing peer-to-peer dialogue related to the skills learned in the workshop will enhance participant understanding and application of the skills learned.

Follow-Up Action Planning

Each agenda in this book, whether half-day, one-day, or two-day, provides an action plan at the conclusion of the workshop to help solidify the learning. These action plans help participants set goals and identify specific actions they can take to apply what they've learned back on the job. One effective technique to ensure that an action plan is taken seriously is to encourage the learner's supervisor to get involved in meaningful ways. Here are a couple of options to consider:

- Ask a high-level manager to kick off each workshop session, either live or through a pre-recorded video, stressing the importance of the action plan.
- Invite different leadership team members throughout the workshop to share their stories about some key competencies and why they are critical to the organization's success. If

leaders are not able to join during the live session, these stories can be included as brief videos or handouts.

- Ask learners to set up a meeting with their supervisors to go over their actions plans as homework after the workshop is completed. Consider providing supervisors with some guiding questions to help facilitate a more meaningful discussion.

For any of these options to be effective, however, supervisors must have a strong understanding of the workshop objectives and content so they are well aware of the competencies, have examined their own strengths and gaps, and empathize with the learner. Supervisors must also be willing to take criticism from the learners because they're likely going to demand more effective communication from others as their own skills continue to grow.

Follow-Up Coaching Sessions

Offering coaching, either in person or virtually, can help learners further develop their communication skills. A coach's role is to be a mirror—to listen and ask questions—that helps those being coached see more clearly their own beliefs, obstacles, and desires. A coach should be completely neutral (supervisors may or may not be the right people to play this role because they are also responsible for reviewing the learner). Outside coaches tend to work best because they may be easier to open up to. The most critical aspect is that the coach be a listener and an asker, not a teller.

EIGHT IDEAS FOR FOLLOW-UP COACHING

1. Define the behavioral objectives desired for change and develop a weekly or biweekly coaching plan so that there is a structured list of topics to discuss consistently.

2. Identify peer-to-peer subgroups to support ongoing communication about the competencies and objectives for behavioral change.

3. Encourage managers and other organizational leaders to incorporate discussions about progress and challenges of the change process in departmental or team meetings.

4. Create specific communication competencies to include in performance expectations.

5. Conduct individual coaching conversations. Supervisors, internal coaches, or external coaches can facilitate these conversations depending on budget considerations.

6. Craft a series of email messages (daily, weekly, or monthly) to deliver to session participants that support the identified competencies and objectives.

7. Revisit the action plans that participants completed during the workshop. These will provide ample discussion centered on behavioral objectives and will promote accountability among participants.

8. Develop an online learning community where participants can hold asynchronous objective-focused discussions, ask questions, and support one another as they work to improve their skills.

Follow-Up Workshops

After your communication skills training sessions are completed, you may find it useful to bring people back together again at three- or six-month intervals. Becoming a stronger, more effective communicator is a very personal journey, and people like to reconnect with and support others who have been through the same thing. Follow-up sessions could be done in person or virtually through teleconferencing, webinars, or other online community tools.

Schedule the first follow-up within three months of the initial workshop for maximum reinforcement of learning. For each follow-up session, create an agenda that encourages participants to discuss challenges they are encountering and share resources they have found to be helpful. Ask learners to bring a sample of their work to discuss (this could be something they are particularly proud of or something that they would like input and help with).

You may have a situation in which the company is willing to invest in significant follow-up. When this is the case, follow up with a half- or full-day workshop. Or try some of the customizing options from chapter 4. A series of one-hour theme-based sessions or Lunch & Learns can be highly effective in tuning up skills and learning new ones.

In addition, encourage supervisors and leaders to attend the follow-up sessions. Recruit them as guest experts or invite them for a lunch or coffee break.

Creating an Open Culture for Effective Communication

Culture change can be a slow and difficult process, and communication style is one of the deepest and most impactful aspects of an organizational culture. The best way to support behavioral change is for employees to see and hear actions and messages from executive leadership and managers that support the ideas communicated during the training program. Workplace leaders must truly model the desired behavior to build trust, or they risk the training program they are paying for quickly losing credibility.

Key Points

- Remember that improving communication skills is a journey—not an event.
- Be creative and consistent. Your commitment to your participants' learning will inspire their own.

- Follow up, with multiple offerings, helps learners implement their action plans and make real progress toward improving behavior and achieving results.

- Management involvement, though difficult to get at first, is critical to organizational change.

What to Do Next

- Select one or two of the follow-up ideas and make a plan to implement them in your next workshop.

- Follow through on your follow-up plan. Demonstrate your commitment to your participants' continued learning by your willingness to continue on the journey with them long after the workshop is completed.

Additional Resource

Olivero, G., K. Bane, and R. Kopelmann. (1997). "Executive Coaching as a Transfer of Training Tool: Effects on Productivity in a Public Agency." *Public Personnel Management* 26(4).

Martin, H.J. (2010). "Improving Training Impact Through Effective Follow-Up: Techniques and Their Application." *Journal of Management Development* 29 (6): 520–534. https://pdfs.semanticscholar.org/2c1c/febd07e-1f761310e7aa221df495021712981.pdf

SECTION IV

WORKSHOP SUPPORTING DOCUMENTS AND ONLINE SUPPORT

Chapter 10
Learning Activities

What's in This Chapter

- Twenty-five learning activities to use in your workshops
- Refer to chapter 13 for instructions to download full-size handouts

To help you facilitate adult learning, we have designed learning activities to deploy regularly throughout the workshop. Their purpose is to challenge and engage learners by breaking up monotony, providing stimulation for different types of learners, and actively helping them acquire new knowledge. Such activities enliven and invigorate the experience, and they help learning stick.

Each learning activity provides detailed information about learning objectives, materials required, timeframe, step-by-step instructions, and variations and debriefing questions if required. Follow the instructions in each learning activity to prepare your workshop agenda, identify and gather materials needed, and successfully guide learners through the activity. The experiences provided by the learning activities help support the topics covered in the workshop. Bonus activities that are not part of the half-, one-, or two-day workshop agendas are also included here. You can use them to modify the existing agenda or to support your own. See chapter 13 for complete instructions on how to download the workshop support materials.

Learning Activities Included in *Communication Skills Virtual Training*

Learning Activity 1: Objective Decision

Learning Activity 2: The Most Difficult Person

Learning Activity 3: Identify the Noise

Learning Activity 4: Impression Improv (created by Sharon Wingron)

Learning Activity 5: Surgical Analysis of Your Story

Learning Activity 6: Listening Is More Than Hearing (created by Ken Phillips)

Learning Activity 7: Listening Stick (Part 1)

Learning Activity 8: Listening Stick (Part 2)

Learning Activity 9: Alpha Beta Exercise

Learning Activity 10: Personal Case Scenario

Learning Activity 11: Document Planning Mind Map

Learning Activity 12: Five Cs

Learning Activity 13: Clear Communication

Learning Activity 14: Concise Communication

Learning Activity 15: Complete Communication

Learning Activity 16: Correct Communication

Learning Activity 17: Considerate Communication: Circles of Influence

Learning Activity 18: Identify Your Reader's Needs

Learning Activity 19: Draft Your Message

Learning Activity 20: Effective Virtual Teams (Part 1) (created by Dawn Mahoney)

Learning Activity 21: Effective Virtual Teams (Part 2) (created by Dawn Mahoney)

Learning Activity 22: 10 Questions About Conflict

Learning Activity 23: Choices (created by Rick Hicks)

Learning Activity 24: Informal Evaluations

Learning Activity 1: Objective Decision

Objective Decision

Objectives

Participants will be able to:

- Independently read and internalize the designed objectives of the workshop.
- Consider and capture their personal objectives and desired learning outcomes.

The objective of this activity also serves to:

- Alleviate the need for the facilitator to begin the workshop with the mundane task of reading the objectives to the class.
- Provide a quick assessment of the learning needs in the class.

Materials

- PowerPoint Slide 2
- Handout 1. Objective Decision
  - Two-day workshop uses Handout 1a
  - One-day workshop uses Handout 1b
  - Half-day workshop uses Handout 1c
- Whiteboard

Time

15 minutes

Instructions

1. Before the workshop begins list all session objectives on a whiteboard.
2. Once the introductions have been completed, present slide 2 on objectives.
3. Instruct the participants refer to Handout 1. Objective Decision and then read and highlight the objectives that are most relevant to them.
4. Once they have completed the task, ask them to use the annotation tools to place a mark next to each objective they highlighted in their handout.

Learning Activity 1, *continued*

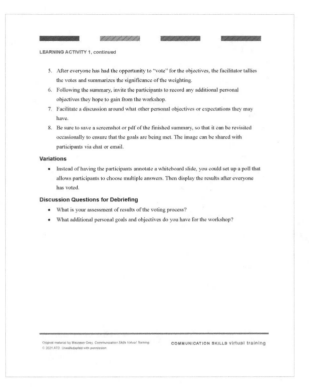

5. After everyone has had the opportunity to "vote" for the objectives, the facilitator tallies the votes and summarizes the significance of the weighting.
6. Following the summary, invite the participants to record any additional personal objectives they hope to gain from the workshop.
7. Facilitate a discussion around what other personal objectives or expectations they may have.
8. Be sure to save a screenshot or pdf of the finished summary, so that it can be revisited occasionally to ensure that the goals are being met. The image can be shared with participants via chat or email.

Variations

- Instead of having the participants annotate a whiteboard slide, you could set up a poll that allows participants to choose multiple answers. Then display the results after everyone has voted.

Discussion Questions for Debriefing

- What is your assessment of results of the voting process?
- What additional personal goals and objectives do you have for the workshop?

Learning Activity 2: The Most Difficult Person

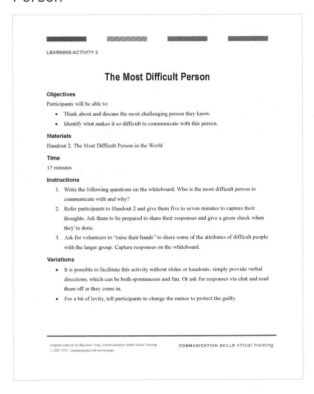

The Most Difficult Person

Objectives

Participants will be able to:

- Think about and discuss the most challenging person they know.
- Identify what makes it so difficult to communicate with this person.

Materials

Handout 2. The Most Difficult Person in the World

Time

15 minutes

Instructions

1. Write the following questions on the whiteboard: Who is the most difficult person to communicate with and why?
2. Refer participants to Handout 2 and give them five to seven minutes to capture their thoughts. Ask them to be prepared to share their responses and give a green check when they're done.
3. Ask for volunteers to "raise their hands" to share some of the attributes of difficult people with the larger group. Capture responses on the whiteboard.

Variations

- It is possible to facilitate this activity without slides or handouts; simply provide verbal directions, which can be both spontaneous and fun. Or ask for responses via chat and read them off as they come in.
- For a bit of levity, tell participants to change the names to protect the guilty.

Learning Activity 2, *continued*

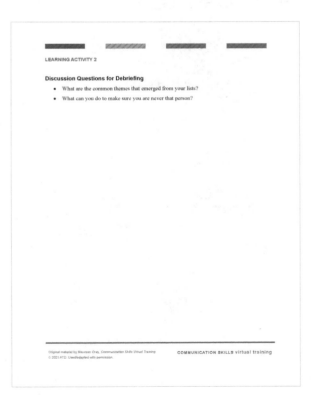

Discussion Questions for Debriefing

- What are the common themes that emerged from your lists?
- What can you do to make sure you are never that person?

Learning Activity 3: Identify the Noise

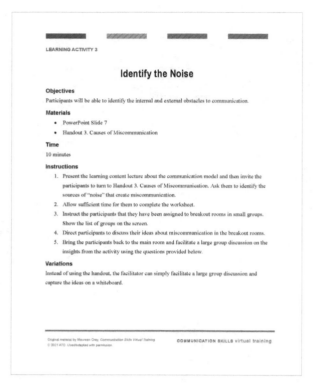

LEARNING ACTIVITY 3

Identify the Noise

Objectives

Participants will be able to identify the internal and external obstacles to communication.

Materials

- PowerPoint Slide 7
- Handout 3. Causes of Miscommunication

Time

10 minutes

Instructions

1. Present the learning content lecture about the communication model and then invite the participants to turn to Handout 3. Causes of Miscommunication. Ask them to identify the sources of "noise" that create miscommunication.
2. Allow sufficient time for them to complete the worksheet.
3. Instruct the participants that they have been assigned to breakout rooms in small groups. Show the list of groups on the screen.
4. Direct participants to discuss their ideas about miscommunication in the breakout rooms.
5. Bring the participants back to the main room and facilitate a large group discussion on the insights from the activity using the questions provided below.

Variations

Instead of using the handout, the facilitator can simply facilitate a large group discussion and capture the ideas on a whiteboard.

Learning Activity 3, *continued*

LEARNING ACTIVITY 3, continued

Discussion Questions for Debriefing

- What are the external sources of noise that get in your way?
- What are the internal sources of noise that get in your way?
- Which of these sources can you control? How can you begin to control them?

Learning Activity 4: Impression Improv (created by Sharon Wingron)

LEARNING ACTIVITY 4

Impression Improv

Objectives

Participants will be able to:

- Identify congruent and incongruent body language.
- Demonstrate the impact of body language in communication.

Materials

- PowerPoint Slide 8
- Handout 5. Impression Improv

Time

15–20 minutes

Instructions

It is important to ensure that tone and body language are congruent with the words we choose when communicating. Sometimes seeing what *not* to do is as powerful (or perhaps more so) than seeing what *to* do! In this activity, participants will have fun demonstrating and identifying what impression a person creates based on a combination of *what they say*, *how* they say it, and *what they do* while saying it.

1. Ask for three volunteers willing to act as the improv actors for this activity. The rest of the group will play the role of audience. Note: Participants in the actor role must have video and audio capability.
2. Invite the audience suggest impressions for the actors to create using the chat feature. They can choose impressions listed in Handout 5 or come up with their own.
3. Instruct the actors to take turns creating the various impressions based on what they say, and more important, how they say it (tone of voice) and what they do (body language, facial expressions, eye contact) while saying it. (Each impression is acted out in fewer than 30 seconds. Only one actor per impression is necessary).

Learning Activity 4, *continued*

LEARNING ACTIVITY 4, continued

4. Ask the audience to observe and note the combination of communication aspects the actor is demonstrating to form the requested impression. Actors should take notes as well. Handout 5 provides a chart to record observations.
5. Close the activity by inviting everyone to discuss their observations, especially congruence among the verbal, vocal, and visual aspects of communication. Use the debrief questions to get the conversation started.

Discussion Questions for Debriefing

- How quickly are impressions formed?
- What does it take to change the observer's mind once the idea is set?
- How do you identify incongruent communication in virtual meeting?
- What are the non-verbal cues you look for to identify congruent and incongruent communication online?

(created by Sharon Wingron, CPTD)

Learning Activity 5: Surgical Analysis of Your Story

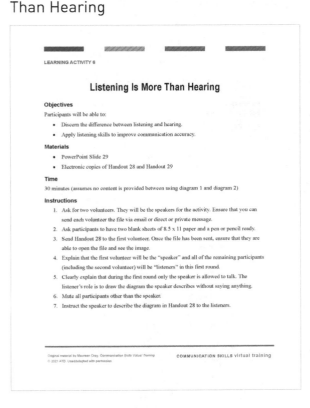

LEARNING ACTIVITY 5

Surgical Analysis of Your Story

Objectives

Participants will be able to

- Identify a difficult situation in the workplace.
- Use the five-step communication awareness model to analyze a challenging conversation.

Materials

- PowerPoint Slides 24 and 25
- Handout 9. Surgical Analysis of Your Story

Time

30–40 minutes

Instructions

1. Ask participants to reflect on a recent or current difficult situation in the workplace.
2. Direct them to analyze that challenging situation by filling out the chart in Handout 9, which will lead them through the five steps of the communication awareness model. The insights they gain from this analysis will help them have a better conversation about the situation in the future.
3. Instruct the participants that they have been assigned to breakout rooms in small groups. Show the list of groups on the screen.
4. Ask them to join their breakout groups to discuss what they have learned about approaching challenging conversations this way.
5. Bring the participants back to the main room and lead a discussion of the activity using the questions below.

Original material by Maureen Orey, *Communication Skills Virtual Training*
© 2021 ATD. Used/adapted with permission.
COMMUNICATION SKILLS virtual training

Learning Activity 5, *continued*

LEARNING ACTIVITY 5, continued

Discussion Questions for Debriefing

- How can you use this tool to have more effective conversations in the future?
- What steps do you need to take to implement this regularly?
- What might get in the way of using this effectively?

Note: The Surgical Analysis Activity is a variation of a concept called the ladder of inference, which was developed by Chris Argyris in 1990.

Original material by Maureen Orey, *Communication Skills Virtual Training*
© 2021 ATD. Used/adapted with permission.
COMMUNICATION SKILLS virtual training

Learning Activity 6: Listening Is More Than Hearing

LEARNING ACTIVITY 6

Listening Is More Than Hearing

Objectives

Participants will be able to:

- Discern the difference between listening and hearing.
- Apply listening skills to improve communication accuracy.

Materials

- PowerPoint Slide 29
- Electronic copies of Handout 28 and Handout 29

Time

30 minutes (assumes no content is provided between using diagram 1 and diagram 2)

Instructions

1. Ask for two volunteers. They will be the speakers for the activity. Ensure that you can send each volunteer the file via email or direct or private message.
2. Ask participants to have two blank sheets of 8.5 x 11 paper and a pen or pencil ready.
3. Send Handout 28 to the first volunteer. Once the file has been sent, ensure that they are able to open the file and see the image.
4. Explain that the first volunteer will be the "speaker" and all of the remaining participants (including the second volunteer) will be "listeners" in this first round.
5. Clearly explain that during the first round only the speaker is allowed to talk. The listener's role is to draw the diagram the speaker describes without saying anything.
6. Mute all participants other than the speaker.
7. Instruct the speaker to describe the diagram in Handout 28 to the listeners.

Original material by Maureen Orey, *Communication Skills Virtual Training*
© 2021 ATD. Used/adapted with permission.
COMMUNICATION SKILLS virtual training

Learning Activity 6, *continued*

LEARNING ACTIVITY 6, continued

8. After everyone is finished, unmute the listeners and display the diagram on the screen. Ask listeners to count the number of triangles they drew correctly. (To be counted as correct, a triangle must be similar in size and position to one on the diagram.)
9. Conduct a quick report out asking participants to post their results in chat. Create a tally on the whiteboard as the responses come in. (Optional approach: use the poll function to tabulate results—especially if it is a larger class.)
10. Announce that you'll now be moving to the second round.
11. Send Handout 29 to the second volunteer and confirm that they can open the file and see the diagram.
12. Explain that the listener's role is now changed and that they are now allowed to speak.
13. Repeat steps 4–9 but skip step 6 because you'll want the listeners to be able to speak.
14. Manage the Q&A and discussion as the participants have questions for the speaker.
15. Facilitate a discussion of the activity using the questions provided.

Variations

- Instead of moving directly into round two (step 10), engage the participants in a discussion of what listening is and what a good listener looks like. This can be done either as a large group discussion or in small groups followed by a report out of what things were discussed. You may even want to record the comments on the whiteboard and use them as a way to define the listener's role in round two.
- Instead of moving directly into round two (step 10), present information on effective listening skills, such as minimal encouragements, open- and close-ended questions, paraphrasing, and summarizing. After covering the material, encourage the listeners in round 2 to use these skills to clarify the speaker's descriptions to draw a more accurate diagram.

Original material by Maureen Orey, *Communication Skills Virtual Training*
© 2021 ATD. Used/adapted with permission.
COMMUNICATION SKILLS virtual training

Learning Activity 6, *continued*

Discussion Questions for Debriefing

- What was the biggest takeaway you got from the role of the listener in round one versus round two?
- What specific listening skills or behaviors did the listeners use in round two to help them draw a more accurate diagram?
- Question for the speaker: How did the interaction in round 2 help you provide more clear directions?

(Created by Ken Phillips)

Learning Activity 6, *continued*

Speaker's Diagram 1
(Handout 28)

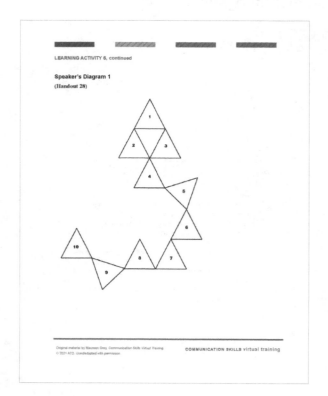

Learning Activity 6, *continued*

Speaker's Diagram 2
(Handout 29)

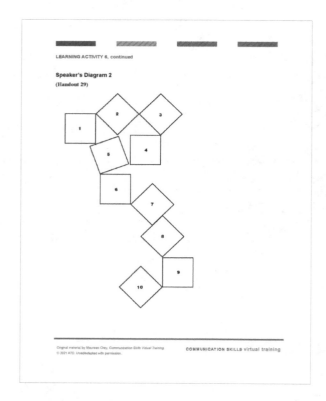

Learning Activity 7: Listening Stick (Part 1)

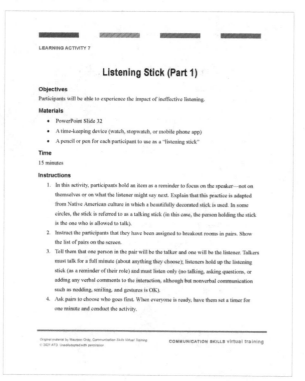

Listening Stick (Part 1)

Objectives

Participants will be able to experience the impact of ineffective listening.

Materials

- PowerPoint Slide 32
- A time-keeping device (watch, stopwatch, or mobile phone app)
- A pencil or pen for each participant to use as a "listening stick"

Time

15 minutes

Instructions

1. In this activity, participants hold an item as a reminder to focus on the speaker—not on themselves or on what the listener might say next. Explain that this practice is adapted from Native American culture in which a beautifully decorated stick is used. In some circles, the stick is referred to as a talking stick (in this case, the person holding the stick is the one who is allowed to talk).
2. Instruct the participants that they have been assigned to breakout rooms in pairs. Show the list of pairs on the screen.
3. Tell them that one person in the pair will be the talker and one will be the listener. Talkers must talk for a full minute (about anything they choose); listeners hold up the listening stick (as a reminder of their role) and must listen only (no talking, asking questions, or adding any verbal comments to the interaction, although but nonverbal communication such as nodding, smiling, and gestures is OK).
4. Ask pairs to choose who goes first. When everyone is ready, have them set a timer for one minute and conduct the activity.

Learning Activity 7, *continued*

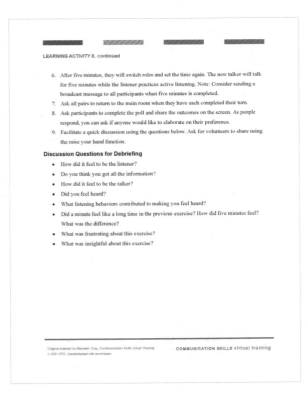

LEARNING ACTIVITY 7, continued

5. After one minute, bring all participants back to the main group and lead a quick discussion using the debrief questions below.
6. Have the pairs return to their breakout rooms and switch roles. The new listeners will now hold the listening stick.
7. Have them set the timer for one minute.
8. After one minute, bring everybody back to the main group, and then facilitate a quick discussion using the questions below.

Discussion Questions for Debriefing

- How did it feel to be the listener?
- Did you feel like you got all the information?
- How did it feel to be the talker?
- Did you feel heard?
- Did a minute feel like a long time? Why?
- What was frustrating about this exercise?

Variation

To streamline the process, skip Steps 5 and 6—instead of bringing all participants back after one minute into the exercise, simply send a message to all groups (via the messaging tool on the platform being used) after the first minute telling everyone to switch roles and continue to Part 2 of the exercise.

Learning Activity 8: Listening Stick (Part 2)

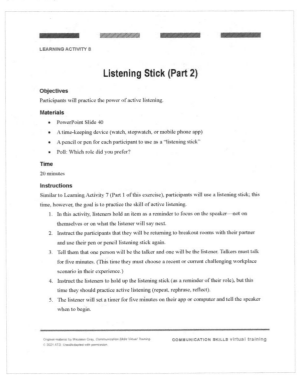

LEARNING ACTIVITY 8

Listening Stick (Part 2)

Objectives

Participants will practice the power of active listening.

Materials

- PowerPoint Slide 40
- A time-keeping device (watch, stopwatch, or mobile phone app)
- A pencil or pen for each participant to use as a "listening stick"
- Poll: Which role did you prefer?

Time

20 minutes

Instructions

Similar to Learning Activity 7 (Part 1 of this exercise), participants will use a listening stick; this time, however, the goal is to practice the skill of active listening.

1. In this activity, listeners hold an item as a reminder to focus on the speaker—not on themselves or on what the listener will say next.
2. Instruct the participants that they will be returning to breakout rooms with their partner and use their pen or pencil listening stick again.
3. Tell them that one person will be the talker and one will be the listener. Talkers must talk for five minutes. (This time they must choose a recent or current challenging workplace scenario in their experience.)
4. Instruct the listeners to hold up the listening stick (as a reminder of their role), but this time they should practice active listening (repeat, rephrase, reflect).
5. The listener will set a timer for five minutes on their app or computer and tell the speaker when to begin.

Learning Activity 8, *continued*

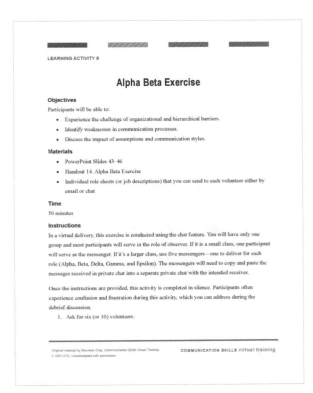

LEARNING ACTIVITY 8, continued

6. After five minutes, they will switch roles and set the time again. The new talker will talk for five minutes while the listener practices active listening. Note: Consider sending a broadcast message to all participants when five minutes is completed.
7. Ask all pairs to return to the main room when they have each completed their turn.
8. Ask participants to complete the poll and share the outcomes on the screen. As people respond, you can ask if anyone would like to elaborate on their preference.
9. Facilitate a quick discussion using the questions below. Ask for volunteers to share using the raise your hand function.

Discussion Questions for Debriefing

- How did it feel to be the listener?
- Do you think you got all the information?
- How did it feel to be the talker?
- Did you feel heard?
- What listening behaviors contributed to making you feel heard?
- Did a minute feel like a long time in the previous exercise? How did five minutes feel? What was the difference?
- What was frustrating about this exercise?
- What was insightful about this exercise?

Learning Activity 9: Alpha Beta Exercise

LEARNING ACTIVITY 9

Alpha Beta Exercise

Objectives

Participants will be able to:

- Experience the challenge of organizational and hierarchical barriers.
- Identify weaknesses in communication processes.
- Discuss the impact of assumptions and communication styles.

Materials

- PowerPoint Slides 43–46
- Handout 14. Alpha Beta Exercise
- Individual role sheets (or job descriptions) that you can send to each volunteer either by email or chat

Time

50 minutes

Instructions

In a virtual delivery, this exercise is conducted using the chat feature. You will have only one group and most participants will serve in the role of observer. If it is a small class, one participant will serve as the messenger. If it's a larger class, use five messengers—one to deliver for each role (Alpha, Beta, Delta, Gamma, and Epsilon). The messengers will need to copy and paste the messages received in private chat into a separate private chat with the intended receiver.

Once the instructions are provided, this activity is completed in silence. Participants often experience confusion and frustration during this activity, which you can address during the debrief discussion.

1. Ask for six (or 10) volunteers.

Learning Activity 9, *continued*

- • Explain that everyone will have a role in the activity but only those six will be differentiated.
2. Present the rules for the activity, which are on Slide 48 and Handout 14.
   - • Solve a simple, analytical problem.
   - • Communicate in writing only.
      - – "You will use the messaging functionality in chat. All messages will be sent to the messenger, who will then distribute only those messages that are formatted properly. The messenger will send properly addressed messages to both the sender and receiver."
   - • No oral communication is permitted.
      - – "Please mute all audio for the duration of the activity. Observers should also turn block their video."
   - • Deliver your messages through chat.
      - – "All messages will be addressed to the intended recipient using the prescribed format, but sent to the messenger for review and forwarding."
      - – "When you believe you have solved the problem, Alpha or Beta will raise a hand and I will check your answer."
3. Assign each volunteer a role (Alpha, Beta, Delta, Gamma, Epsilon, and messenger) that is known to the entire group.
   - • Send each player their individual and confidential job description file.
4. Send the observer job description to the remaining participants.
5. Explain that the remainder of the audience will be observers.
6. Present the process for communication for this activity using Slides 49 and 50 (and Handout 14):
   - • Only written communication allowed.
   - • All communication is sent by direct chat to the messenger for distribution. (Do not send to "all participants.")

Learning Activity 9, *continued*

- • Improperly addressed mail will be returned or ignored.
- • Communication can only go through the approved channels (see the diagram on Slide 49).
7. Reiterate that the goal of the activity is for the team to "solve a simple, analytical problem." This is the extent of direction that the team will receive.
8. Tell participants that the activity is likely to go on for about 30 minutes. Before starting, give everyone five minutes (set a timer) to get familiar with their roles, ensure they have what they need, and get ready to start.
9. Remind all observers to hide their video and tell everyone to mute their audio before starting the activity.
10. Use Slide 51 and the debrief questions to help facilitate a discussion of what the participants learned from the activity. This discussion can be incredibly rich; encourage participants to capture their insights on Handout 14.

Discussion Questions for Debriefing

- • Ask for a show of hands/green check marks to see how many team members were told the goal of the project.
- • Then ask Alpha and Beta if they knew the goal of the project.
- • Ask Alpha and Beta if they knew who told your team the goal of the project.
- • What were your observations about Alpha and Beta?
- • What were your observations about Gamma, Delta, and Epsilon?
- • What did you notice about the written communication?
- • What was frustrating about this experience?
- • How is this like real life within an organization?

Learning Activity 9, *continued*

Alpha Beta Activity

Instructions for Alpha ((Confidential))

In this exercise, you are Alpha. The reporting structure is as follows: Beta reports to you; communicate with Beta only through the exchange of written notes (chat). Beta may exchange notes with you and Gamma, Delta, and Epsilon, who may exchange notes with Beta only. No other communication is permitted.

- • There are six familiar symbols.
- • Each person has five of the six symbols.
- • There are four copies of the five symbols.
- • There are five copies of one of the symbols.
- • Your objective is to determine which one symbol all five people hold.

Your Symbols:

Learning Activity 9, *continued*

Alpha Beta Activity

Instructions for Beta ((Confidential))

- • Alpha and Beta may exchange notes (chat).
- • Gamma, Delta, and Epsilon may exchange notes with Beta only.
- • No other communication is permitted.
- • There are five symbols below. You may not show them to anyone.
- • If you have any questions, raise your hand.

Your Symbols:

Learning Activity 9, *continued*

Alpha Beta Activity

Instructions for Gamma ((Confidential))

- Alpha and Beta may exchange notes (chat).
- Gamma, Delta, and Epsilon may exchange notes with Beta only.
- No other communication is permitted.
- There are five symbols below.
- You may not show them to anyone.
- If you have any questions, raise your hand.

Your Symbols:

Learning Activity 9, *continued*

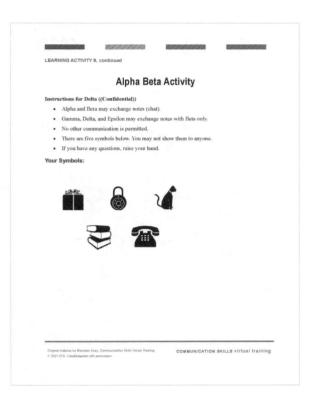

Alpha Beta Activity

Instructions for Delta ((Confidential))

- Alpha and Beta may exchange notes (chat).
- Gamma, Delta, and Epsilon may exchange notes with Beta only.
- No other communication is permitted.
- There are five symbols below. You may not show them to anyone.
- If you have any questions, raise your hand.

Your Symbols:

Learning Activity 9, *continued*

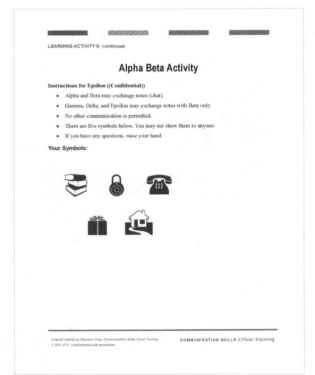

Alpha Beta Activity

Instructions for Epsilon ((Confidential))

- Alpha and Beta may exchange notes (chat).
- Gamma, Delta, and Epsilon may exchange notes with Beta only.
- No other communication is permitted.
- There are five symbols below. You may not show them to anyone.
- If you have any questions, raise your hand.

Your Symbols:

Learning Activity 9, *continued*

Alpha Beta Activity

Instructions for Messenger ((Confidential))

- Deliver any messages that are properly addressed to their intended receiver.
- You will need to copy and paste the messages received in private chat and then send them to the intended receiver also via private chat.
- Do not deliver messages that aren't properly addressed.
- If a message is not addressed properly, either:
  - Give it back to the sender.
  - Delete it.
- Move as rapidly as you can.
- If you have any questions, raise your hand.

Learning Activity 9, *continued*

Learning Activity 10: Personal Case Scenario

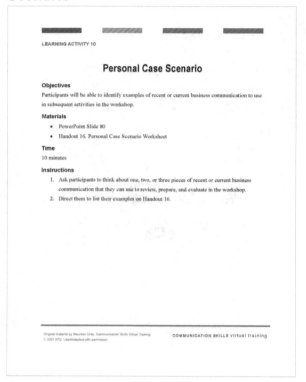

Learning Activity 11: Document Planning Mind Map

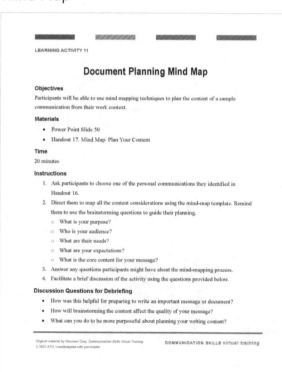

Learning Activity 12: Five Cs

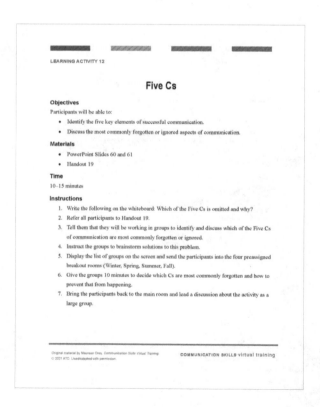

Learning Activity 12, *continued*

LEARNING ACTIVITY 12, continued

Discussion Questions for Debriefing
- What did you identify as the most commonly forgotten or ignored aspects of communication?
- What similarities or differences are there between the groups?
- What solutions did your team identify to fix this problem?

Original material by Maureen Orey, *Communication Skills Virtual Training*
© 2021 ATD. Used/adapted with permission.

COMMUNICATION SKILLS virtual training

Learning Activity 13: Clear Communication

LEARNING ACTIVITY 13

Clear Communication

Objectives
Participants will practice writing with clarity.

Materials
- PowerPoint Slide 62
- Handout 20. Practical Practice—Clear Communication

Time
25 minutes

Instructions
1. Instruct the participants that they have been assigned to breakout rooms in pairs. Show the list of pairs on the screen.
2. Describe this scenario to the participants: A Martian ship has landed on Earth, and the Martians are here to learn Earthly customs and procedures. While the Martians can read English, they know nothing else about our customs.
3. Ask your participants to write instructions for a common human task—such as brushing teeth, combing hair, or getting dressed—so the Martians can start practicing a healthy human habit. Instruct them to use Handout 20 to record their work.
4. Remind them to do their best to follow the guidelines for all five Cs (clear, concise, complete, correct, considerate), focusing especially on clarity.
5. Direct them to exchange the instructions they've written with their partners to check each other's work.
6. Bring the participants back to the main room and ask them to share their instructions with the class. Discuss the activity using the questions provided.

Original material by Maureen Orey, *Communication Skills Virtual Training*
© 2021 ATD. Used/adapted with permission.

COMMUNICATION SKILLS virtual training

Learning Activity 13, *continued*

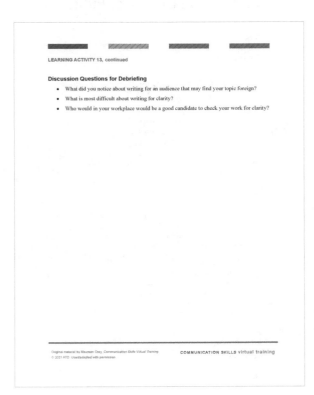

LEARNING ACTIVITY 13, continued

Discussion Questions for Debriefing
- What did you notice about writing for an audience that may find your topic foreign?
- What is most difficult about writing for clarity?
- Who would in your workplace would be a good candidate to check your work for clarity?

Original material by Maureen Orey, *Communication Skills Virtual Training*
© 2021 ATD. Used/adapted with permission.

COMMUNICATION SKILLS virtual training

Learning Activity 14: Concise Communication

LEARNING ACTIVITY 14

Concise Communication

Objectives
Participants will be able to rewrite and eliminate wordy expressions.

Materials
- PowerPoint Slide 63
- Handout 21. Practical Practice—Concise Communication

Time
15 minutes

Instructions
1. Being concise means saying what you have to say in the fewest possible words without sacrificing the other "C" attributes. A concise message is complete without being wordy and saves time and expense for both you and the reader.
2. Instruct the participants that they have been assigned to breakout rooms in pairs. Show the list of pairs on the screen.
3. Direct them to complete the exercises in Handout 21.
4. Remind them to do their best to include the guidelines for all Five Cs (clear, concise, complete, correct, considerate), focusing especially on being concise.
5. Direct them to exchange their worksheets with their partners to check each other's work.
6. After 10 minutes, bring everybody back to the main group, and facilitate a quick discussion using the questions below.

Discussion Questions for Debriefing
- What is most difficult about writing concisely?
- What did you eliminate first?
- How did you determine what to eliminate?

Original material by Maureen Orey, *Communication Skills Virtual Training*
© 2021 ATD. Used/adapted with permission.

COMMUNICATION SKILLS virtual training

Learning Activity 15: Complete Communication

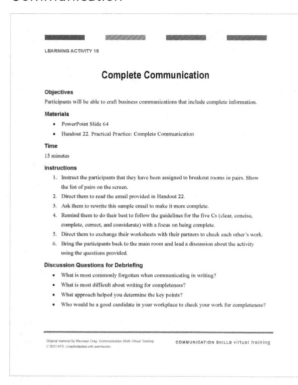

LEARNING ACTIVITY 15

Complete Communication

Objectives

Participants will be able to craft business communications that include complete information.

Materials

- PowerPoint Slide 64
- Handout 22. Practical Practice: Complete Communication

Time

15 minutes

Instructions

1. Instruct the participants that they have been assigned to breakout rooms in pairs. Show the list of pairs on the screen.
2. Direct them to read the email provided in Handout 22.
3. Ask them to rewrite this sample email to make it more complete.
4. Remind them to do their best to follow the guidelines for the five Cs (clear, concise, complete, correct, and considerate) with a focus on being complete.
5. Direct them to exchange their worksheets with their partners to check each other's work.
6. Bring the participants back to the main room and lead a discussion about the activity using the questions provided.

Discussion Questions for Debriefing

- What is most commonly forgotten when communicating in writing?
- What is most difficult about writing for completeness?
- What approach helped you determine the key points?
- Who would be a good candidate in your workplace to check your work for completeness?

Learning Activity 16: Correct Communication

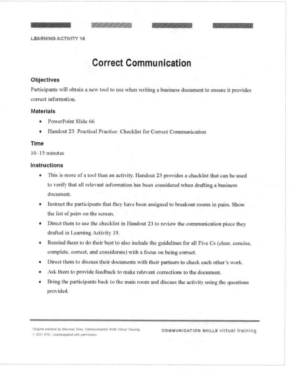

LEARNING ACTIVITY 16

Correct Communication

Objectives

Participants will obtain a new tool to use when writing a business document to ensure it provides correct information.

Materials

- PowerPoint Slide 66
- Handout 23. Practical Practice: Checklist for Correct Communication

Time

10–15 minutes

Instructions

- This is more of a tool than an activity. Handout 23 provides a checklist that can be used to verify that all relevant information has been considered when drafting a business document.
- Instruct the participants that they have been assigned to breakout rooms in pairs. Show the list of pairs on the screen.
- Direct them to use the checklist in Handout 23 to review the communication piece they drafted in Learning Activity 19.
- Remind them to do their best to also include the guidelines for all Five Cs (clear, concise, complete, correct, and considerate) with a focus on being correct.
- Direct them to discuss their documents with their partners to check each other's work.
- Ask them to provide feedback to make relevant corrections to the document.
- Bring the participants back to the main room and discuss the activity using the questions provided.

Learning Activity 16, *continued*

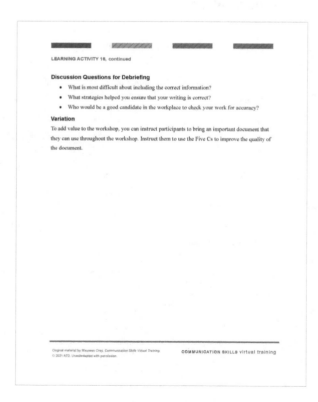

LEARNING ACTIVITY 16, continued

Discussion Questions for Debriefing

- What is most difficult about including the correct information?
- What strategies helped you ensure that your writing is correct?
- Who would be a good candidate in the workplace to check your work for accuracy?

Variation

To add value to the workshop, you can instruct participants to bring an important document that they can use throughout the workshop. Instruct them to use the Five Cs to improve the quality of the document.

Learning Activity 17: Considerate Communication: Circles of Influence

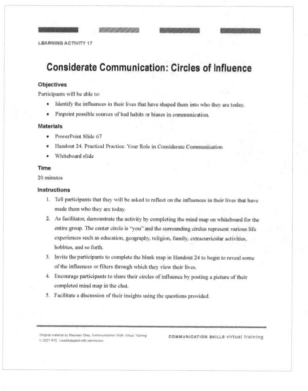

LEARNING ACTIVITY 17

Considerate Communication: Circles of Influence

Objectives

Participants will be able to:

- Identify the influences in their lives that have shaped them into who they are today.
- Pinpoint possible sources of bad habits or biases in communication.

Materials

- PowerPoint Slide 67
- Handout 24. Practical Practice: Your Role in Considerate Communication
- Whiteboard slide

Time

20 minutes

Instructions

1. Tell participants that they will be asked to reflect on the influences in their lives that have made them who they are today.
2. As facilitator, demonstrate the activity by completing the mind map on whiteboard for the entire group. The center circle is "you" and the surrounding circles represent various life experiences such as education, geography, religion, family, extracurricular activities, hobbies, and so forth.
3. Invite the participants to complete the blank map in Handout 24 to begin to reveal some of the influences or filters through which they view their lives.
4. Encourage participants to share their circles of influence by posting a picture of their completed mind map in the chat.
5. Facilitate a discussion of their insights using the questions provided.

Learning Activity 17, *continued*

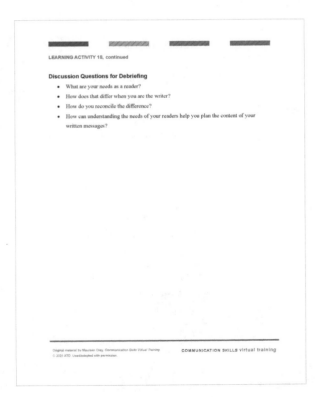

LEARNING ACTIVITY 17, continued

Discussion Questions for Debriefing
- What are your observations about yourself as a result of this exercise?
- Often when we meet people, we realize quickly that we either like them or we don't. Why do you think that is?
- The circles of influence mind map represents a filter through which we see life. How often do you "clean your filter"?
- How can these perspectives change the way you communicate with others to be more considerate?

Variations
- This activity can be facilitated as an impromptu exercise with little or no preparation. The facilitator can simply draw the mind map on a blank whiteboard slide with an annotation tool to demonstrate the model, and participants can use a blank sheet of paper.
- This exercise can be very effective when discussing diversity, the origin of conscious and unconscious biases and belief systems, and their impact on communication and conflict.

Original material by Maureen Orey, Communication Skills Virtual Training © 2021 ATD. Used/adapted with permission.   **COMMUNICATION SKILLS virtual training**

Learning Activity 18: Identify Your Reader's Needs

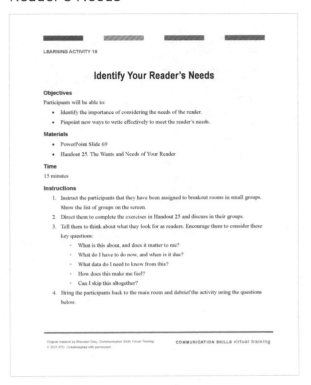

LEARNING ACTIVITY 18

Identify Your Reader's Needs

Objectives
Participants will be able to:
- Identify the importance of considering the needs of the reader.
- Pinpoint new ways to write effectively to meet the reader's needs.

Materials
- PowerPoint Slide 69
- Handout 25. The Wants and Needs of Your Reader

Time
15 minutes

Instructions
1. Instruct the participants that they have been assigned to breakout rooms in small groups. Show the list of groups on the screen.
2. Direct them to complete the exercises in Handout 25 and discuss in their groups.
3. Tell them to think about what they look for as readers. Encourage them to consider these key questions:
   - What is this about, and does it matter to me?
   - What do I have to do now, and when is it due?
   - What data do I need to know from this?
   - How does this make me feel?
   - Can I skip this altogether?
4. Bring the participants back to the main room and debrief the activity using the questions below.

Original material by Maureen Orey, Communication Skills Virtual Training © 2021 ATD. Used/adapted with permission.   **COMMUNICATION SKILLS virtual training**

Learning Activity 18, *continued*

LEARNING ACTIVITY 18, continued

Discussion Questions for Debriefing
- What are your needs as a reader?
- How does that differ when you are the writer?
- How do you reconcile the difference?
- How can understanding the needs of your readers help you plan the content of your written messages?

Original material by Maureen Orey, Communication Skills Virtual Training © 2021 ATD. Used/adapted with permission.   **COMMUNICATION SKILLS virtual training**

Learning Activity 19: Draft Your Message

LEARNING ACTIVITY 19

Draft Your Message

Objectives
Participants will be able to draft a document that considers the needs of the reader and conforms to the Five Cs (clear, considerate, complete, correct, and considerate).

Materials
- PowerPoint Slide 70
- Handout 26. Draft Your Message
- Examples from Handout 16. Personal Case Scenarios

Time
30 minutes

Instructions
1. Instruct the participants that they have been assigned to breakout rooms in pairs. Show the list of pairs on the screen.
2. Ask participants to choose a personal case scenario from Handout 16 to draft a real communication piece that they will deliver in the near future.
3. Instruct them to draft the message on Handout 26, applying what they have learned about addressing the needs of the reader and implementing the Five Cs (clear, concise, complete, correct, considerate).
4. Direct them to exchange their worksheets with a partner to review each other's work (quality check) and provide feedback.
5. Bring the participants back to the main room and lead a discussion of the activity using the questions provided.

Original material by Maureen Orey, Communication Skills Virtual Training © 2021 ATD. Used/adapted with permission.   **COMMUNICATION SKILLS virtual training**

Learning Activity 19, *continued*

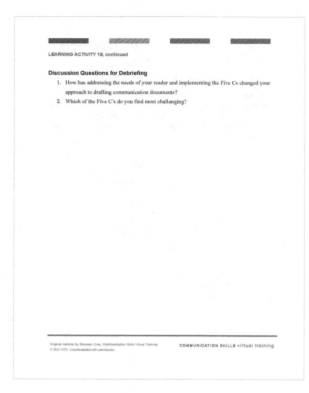

Discussion Questions for Debriefing

1. How has addressing the needs of your reader and implementing the Five Cs changed your approach to drafting communication documents?
2. Which of the Five C's do you find most challenging?

COMMUNICATION SKILLS virtual training

Learning Activity 20: Effective Virtual Teams (Part 1)

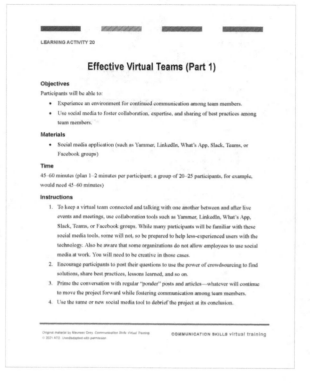

Effective Virtual Teams (Part 1)

Objectives

Participants will be able to:

- Experience an environment for continued communication among team members.
- Use social media to foster collaboration, expertise, and sharing of best practices among team members.

Materials

- Social media application (such as Yammer, LinkedIn, What's App, Slack, Teams, or Facebook groups)

Time

45–60 minutes (plan 1–2 minutes per participant; a group of 20–25 participants, for example, would need 45–60 minutes)

Instructions

1. To keep a virtual team connected and talking with one another between and after live events and meetings, use collaboration tools such as Yammer, LinkedIn, What's App, Slack, Teams, or Facebook groups. While many participants will be familiar with these social media tools, some will not, so be prepared to help less-experienced users with the technology. Also be aware that some organizations do not allow employees to use social media at work. You will need to be creative in those cases.
2. Encourage participants to post their questions to use the power of crowdsourcing to find solutions, share best practices, lessons learned, and so on.
3. Prime the conversation with regular "ponder" posts and articles—whatever will continue to move the project forward while fostering communication among team members.
4. Use the same or new social media tool to debrief the project at its conclusion.

COMMUNICATION SKILLS virtual training

Learning Activity 20, *continued*

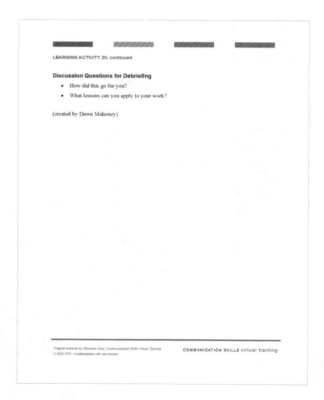

Discussion Questions for Debriefing

- How did this go for you?
- What lessons can you apply to your work?

(created by Dawn Mahoney)

COMMUNICATION SKILLS virtual training

Learning Activity 21: Effective Virtual Teams (Part 2)

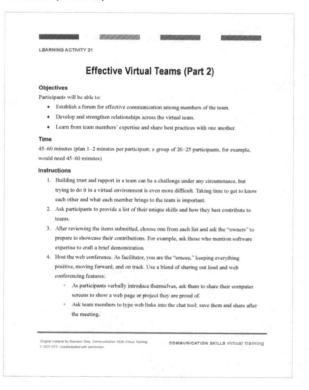

Effective Virtual Teams (Part 2)

Objectives

Participants will be able to:

- Establish a forum for effective communication among members of the team.
- Develop and strengthen relationships across the virtual team.
- Learn from team members' expertise and share best practices with one another.

Time

45–60 minutes (plan 1–2 minutes per participant; a group of 20–25 participants, for example, would need 45–60 minutes)

Instructions

1. Building trust and rapport in a team can be a challenge under any circumstance, but trying to do it in a virtual environment is even more difficult. Taking time to get to know each other and what each member brings to the team is important.
2. Ask participants to provide a list of their unique skills and how they best contribute to teams.
3. After reviewing the items submitted, choose one from each list and ask the "owners" to prepare to showcase their contributions. For example, ask those who mention software expertise to craft a brief demonstration.
4. Host the web conference. As facilitator, you are the "emcee," keeping everything positive, moving forward, and on track. Use a blend of sharing out loud and web conferencing features:
   - As participants verbally introduce themselves, ask them to share their computer screens to show a web page or project they are proud of.
   - Ask team members to type web links into the chat tool; save them and share after the meeting.

COMMUNICATION SKILLS virtual training

Learning Activity 21, *continued*

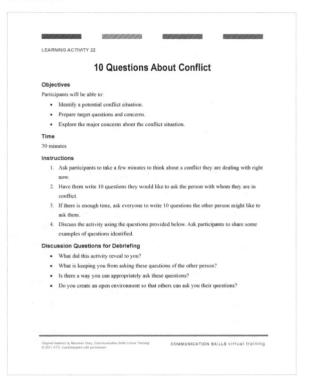

LEARNING ACTIVITY 21, continued

- Create a whiteboard for each participant who presents. Invite them to post information they will be sharing with the group there. Flip to each whiteboard as team members introduce themselves.
5. Facilitate a discussion about the activity using the questions below.

Variations
- Use this as an opening icebreaker activity for the workshop.
- Create breakout rooms and have the teams share their unique skills and how they could be leveraged collectively to develop a super star team.

Discussion Questions for Debriefing
- What about doing this event was helpful to you?
- Who do you feel you will be able to contact right away?
- What similarities among team members were uncovered?
- What differences among team members were uncovered?
- How might you use what you've learned to build a cohesive, productive team?

(Created by Dawn Mahoney)

Learning Activity 22: 10 Questions About Conflict

LEARNING ACTIVITY 22

10 Questions About Conflict

Objectives
Participants will be able to:
- Identify a potential conflict situation.
- Prepare target questions and concerns.
- Explore the major concerns about the conflict situation.

Time
30 minutes

Instructions
1. Ask participants to take a few minutes to think about a conflict they are dealing with right now.
2. Have them write 10 questions they would like to ask the person with whom they are in conflict.
3. If there is enough time, ask everyone to write 10 questions the other person might like to ask them.
4. Discuss the activity using the questions provided below. Ask participants to share some examples of questions identified.

Discussion Questions for Debriefing
- What did this activity reveal to you?
- What is keeping you from asking these questions of the other person?
- Is there a way you can appropriately ask these questions?
- Do you create an open environment so that others can ask you their questions?

Learning Activity 23: Choices

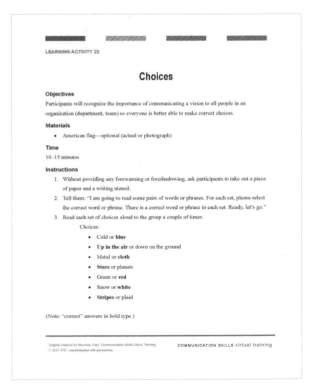

LEARNING ACTIVITY 23

Choices

Objectives
Participants will recognize the importance of communicating a vision to all people in an organization (department, team) so everyone is better able to make correct choices.

Materials
- American flag—optional (actual or photograph)

Time
10–15 minutes

Instructions
1. Without providing any forewarning or foreshadowing, ask participants to take out a piece of paper and a writing utensil.
2. Tell them: "I am going to read some pairs of words or phrases. For each set, please select the correct word or phrase. There is a correct word or phrase in each set. Ready, let's go."
3. Read each set of choices aloud to the group a couple of times:
   Choices:
   - Cold or **blue**
   - **Up in the air** or down on the ground
   - Metal or **cloth**
   - **Stars** or planets
   - Green or **red**
   - Snow or **white**
   - **Stripes** or plaid

(Note: "correct" answers in bold type.)

Learning Activity 23, *continued*

LEARNING ACTIVITY 23, continued

1. Answer questions by simply repeating: "Write down the correct answer." This will frustrate some people, but that's OK. That emotion can become a good debriefing point at the end of the activity.
2. After you have finished reading the choices, ask for volunteers to share their answers and then tell them how many correct answers they chose (the words in bold type in step 3).
3. Conduct a quick discussion about how people felt (for example, frustrated, confused, didn't make sense, and so on). The learning point here is that people get frustrated when they don't understand where they are going or don't have the complete picture.
4. Ask if anybody knows the answer. Often one or two people will have figured it out. If not, ask people to sit back and visualize the American flag (or you can simply show actual flag or photo of one).
5. Now quickly run through the choices again, this time with the whole class responding out loud.
6. Facilitate a discussion of the activity using the questions provided.

Discussion Questions for Debriefing
- How easy is it to make the choices when everyone shares the same vision?
- How can we create a common vision back in our workplaces (projects, teams, and so on)?
- How clear do we need to be to communicate our vision to all employees?
- How can sharing vision enable others to make more complex decisions?
- How does aligning decisions with the vision help people make the "right" choices?

Variations
- This activity is effective in facilitating other kinds of training as well, such as strategic planning, performance development, leadership, or teambuilding.
- When facilitating international groups or training in a country outside the United States, change the choices to reflect features of the participants' country flag.

(Created by Rick Hicks © 1995, 2014 Rick Hicks.)

Learning Activity 24: Informal Evaluations

Learning Activity 24, *continued*

Informal Evaluations

Objectives

Participants will be able to provide informal and anonymous mid-session feedback to the facilitator. The objective of this activity also serves to:

- Alleviate the need for a formal mid-session evaluation form.
- Provide a quick pulse check of the satisfaction levels and needs of the class.

Materials

- On-screen whiteboard
- Annotation tools enabled for participants
- Virtual sticky notes (using online collaboration tools such as Mural.com or Miro.com)
- Chat stream (in your online platform such as Teams, Zoom, or WebEx)

Time

5 minutes

Instructions

Here are several techniques and activities to gather informal feedback using virtual collaboration tools mid-session or at the end of a module.

Red Light, Green Light

1. On the left side of the page, place a graphic of a traffic light.
2. Instruct the participants to use the virtual sticky notes to share any ideas about what is going well (green light), what's just okay (yellow light), and what needs to be improved (red light).
3. Invite them to place their virtual sticky note nearest to the appropriate color on the traffic light before they leave the session for the day.

On a Scale of 1 to 5

1. Ask participants to think back over the first part of the workshop. Instruct them to identify a number from 1 to 5 (1 = poor and 5 = excellent) to rate how well they think the workshop is going so far.
2. Instruct the participants to put their rating into chat.
3. Invite them to provide any additional notes or comments to support the rating.

Plus/Delta

1. Place a vertical line down the middle of the page. Draw a "+" on the top left side of the page and draw a triangle (delta) on the top right side.
2. Instruct the participants to use virtual sticky notes to share any ideas about what is going well (+) what needs to be changed or improved (delta).
3. Invite them to place the sticky note nearest to the appropriate column on the chart as they leave the session.

Note: this activity can also be facilitated using a whiteboard and annotation tools.

Chapter 11

Assessments

What's in This Chapter

- Ten assessments to use in your workshops in thumbnail format for reference
- To pre-work or not to pre-work, that is the question
- Refer to chapter 13 for instructions to download full-size assessments

---

Assessments and evaluations are critical to a workshop—before it begins, as it goes on, and when it concludes. To prepare an effective workshop for participants, you have to assess their needs and those of their organization. Although a formal needs analysis is outside the scope of this book, the needs analysis assessments in this chapter can help you identify important information about the expectations for the workshop—both of the organization and of the participants—and about what participants' current knowledge or skill level of the topic may be. This information can help you make course adjustments to fit the needs of the learners and their organization.

Using assessments during the workshop helps participants identify areas of strength and weakness, enabling them to capitalize on their strengths and improve their weaknesses to be able to perform better in the workplace. Assessments can also be used during the workshop to check in on participants' learning so that you can make any needed adjustments as you go.

Finally, evaluation assessments of the workshop and the facilitator are vital both for the organization and for you as the facilitator. To learn if you met the goals and expectations, you want direct responses from participants. Although negative comments can be tough to read, ultimately they allow you to continually learn and improve your skills as a learning facilitator.

The instruments in this chapter provide instructions on how to complete each assessment and when to use it in the course of the workshop, as well as an explanation of the assessment's purpose. See chapter 13 for complete instructions on how to download the workshop assessment instruments.

To Pre-Work or Not to Pre-Work . . .

One of the most common uses of assessments is as pre-work before a workshop event. And yet there seems to be a never-ending discussion about whether or not pre-work is beneficial. On one hand, pre-work can build interest among participants, increase personal investment in the training, and connect participants with the facilitator and others in the workshop. On the other hand, the pressures of the workplace make it a certainty that at least some of your participants won't complete it. Then what do you do?

Many of the assessments offered here are designed to be short enough to complete during the workshop, and you can incorporate them easily into the flow of your workshop agenda. There is one exception to this: Assessment 2: Communication Style Inventory (CSI), courtesy of Ken Phillips of Phillips Associates, which is longer and more robust than may be easily conducted during the workshop. With a long assessment such as the CSI, it may be better to ask the participants to complete it prior to coming to class. It would also work well as a homework assignment between sessions or as a post-workshop activity. When you do assign pre-work, help your participants understand that the assessment adds value to the workshop experience. You will want to create a sense of urgency and an expectation for completion. Sometimes it is even helpful to incentivize your participants.

Assessments Included in *Communication Skills Virtual Training*

Assessment 1. Listening Behavior Assessment

Assessment 2. Communication Style Inventory

Assessment 3. Course Evaluation

Assessment 4. Facilitator Competencies

Assessment 5. Interpersonal Skills

Assessment 6. Learning Needs Assessment Sheet

Assessment 7. Needs Analysis Discussion Form

Assessment 8. Nonverbal Communication Self-Assessment

Assessment 9. Skills Application Reflection

Assessment 10. Skills Mastery Assessment

Assessment 1: Listening Behavior Assessment

ASSESSMENT 1

Listening Behavior Assessment

How Good Are My Listening Skills?

Instructions: This assessment helps you learn what it takes to be a good listener and then helps you create an action plan to improve your listening skills. Place a ✓ in one of the boxes to the right of each item, depending on how you see yourself today. No one will see your ratings unless you share them, so please be honest with yourself.

Listening Behaviors

When another person is speaking to me, I...	Always	Frequently	Sometimes	Rarely	Never
1. Focus on the speaker as much as possible.					
2. Concentrate on content of the message.					
3. Anticipate what the speaker is going to say.					
4. Establish eye contact with the speaker.					
5. Keep listening even if I disagree with the speaker.					
6. Nod, smile, or give other nonverbal cues.					
7. Plan my response in my head.					
8. Get distracted by environmental sounds.					
9. Take notes if necessary to help me remember.					
10. Listen without judging or critiquing.					
11. Interrupt the speaker before they are done.					
12. Think about issues unrelated to the topic.					
13. Pay attention to the speaker's nonverbal communication.					

Original material by Maureen Orey, *Communication Skills Virtual Training.*
© 2021 ATD. Used/adapted with permission.

COMMUNICATION SKILLS virtual training

Assessment 1, *continued*

ASSESSMENT 1, continued

When another person is speaking to me, I...	Always	Frequently	Sometimes	Rarely	Never
14. Restate the speaker's message in my own words.					
15. Adapt my response to fit the situation.					
16. Differentiate between fact and opinion.					
17. Look like I'm listening when I'm not.					
18. Ask questions to gain clarity about the message.					
19. React emotionally to the speaker's message.					
20. Consider how the speaker may react to my response.					
21. Clarify the meaning of the speaker's words if I'm unsure about definitions.					
22. Allow speaker to vent their frustration.					
23. Think of different views on the topic.					
24. Display an open and caring posture.					
25. Create a nonthreatening environment.					

How to Understand the Assessment Results

If you responded "always," "frequently," or "sometimes" for items 3, 7, 8, 11, 12, 17, or 19, you need to improve your listening behaviors in these areas, especially your focus on the speaker and how you filter information.

If you responded with "sometimes," "rarely," or "never" for items 5, 6, 13, 14, 15, 20, and 23, which directly relate to providing feedback to the speaker effectively during a conversation, consider adding these areas to your action plan to improve your listening behaviors.

Original material by Maureen Orey, *Communication Skills Virtual Training.*
© 2021 ATD. Used/adapted with permission.

COMMUNICATION SKILLS virtual training

Assessment 2: Communication Style Inventory (22 pages)

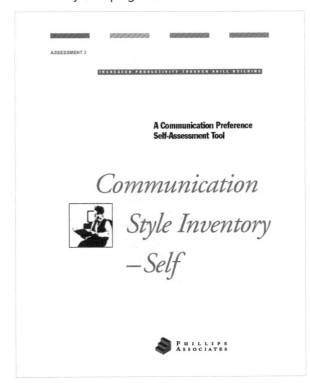

ASSESSMENT 2

INCREASED PRODUCTIVITY THROUGH SKILL BUILDING

A Communication Preference Self-Assessment Tool

Communication Style Inventory —Self

PHILLIPS ASSOCIATES

Assessment 3: Course Evaluation

ASSESSMENT 3

Course Evaluation

Course: _____
Date: _____

What did I learn that I will be able to use right away?
_____

Were the course objectives met?   ☐ Yes   ☐ No

Comments:
_____

Please circle a number for each of the following questions:

	Needs Improvement	Could Be Better	Good	Very Good	Exceptional	N/A
Was the instructor knowledgeable?	1	2	3	4	5	n/a
Was the classroom instruction effective?	1	2	3	4	5	n/a
Was there enough group work?	1	2	3	4	5	n/a
Was the content helpful to me?	1	2	3	4	5	n/a
How were the course materials?	1	2	3	4	5	n/a
How was the facility?	1	2	3	4	5	n/a

Was the pace of the course: ☐ Too slow   ☐ Just right   ☐ Too fast

Additional comments or topic recommendations:
_____
_____

Original material by Maureen Orey, *Communication Skills Virtual Training.*
© 2021 ATD. Used/adapted with permission.

COMMUNICATION SKILLS virtual training

ASSESSMENT 4

Facilitator Competencies

This assessment instrument will help you as the facilitator manage your professional development and increase the effectiveness of your communication skills training sessions. You can use this instrument in the following ways:

- **Self-assessment.** Use the assessment to rate yourself on the five-point scale, which will generate an overall profile and help determine the competency areas that are in the greatest need of improvement.
- **End-of-course feedback.** Honest feedback from the training participants can lessen the possibility that facilitators deceive themselves about the 12 competencies. Trainees may not be able to rate the facilitator on all 12, so it may be necessary to ask the participants to rate only those they consider themselves qualified to address.
- **Observer feedback.** Facilitators may observe one another's training sessions and provide highly useful information on the 12 competencies that are crucial to be effective in conducting training.
- **Repeat ratings.** This assessment can be the basis for tracking professional growth on the competencies needed to be an effective facilitator. The repeat measure may be obtained as often as needed to gauge progress on action plans for improvement.

The Competencies

Facilitators are faced with challenges anytime they lead a training session. Many skills are necessary to help participants meet their learning needs and to ensure that the organization achieves its desired results for the training. This assessment contains a set of 12 important competencies that effective communication skills training requires. Not all seasoned facilitators have expertise in all these competencies, but they may represent learning and growth areas for almost any facilitator.

Here is a detailed explanation of the importance of each of the dozen crucial elements of facilitator competence.

Understanding Adult Learners
Uses knowledge of the principles of adult learning in both designing and delivering training.

Effective facilitators are able to draw on the experiences of the learners in a training session and then give them the applicable content and tools to

---

ASSESSMENT 4, continued

engage them fully and help them see the value of the learning. It is also important to provide learners with opportunities to solve problems and think critically so they can work through real business issues and develop additional skills.

Presentation Skills
Presents content clearly to achieve the desired outcomes of the training. Encourages learners to generate their own answers through effectively leading group discussions.

Of all the competencies a facilitator uses during a training session, none may be more obvious than the need to have exceptional presentation skills. The facilitator's ability to present content effectively and in an entertaining way is one of the first things learners notice and is a large part of a successful workshop. The nature of adult learning makes it equally important that the facilitator is not just a talking head but is also adept at initiating, drawing out, guiding, and summarizing information gleaned from large-group discussions during a training session. The facilitator's role is not to feed answers to learners as if they are empty vessels waiting to be filled. Rather, it is the facilitator's primary task to generate learning on the part of the participants through their own process of discovery.

Communication Skills
Expresses self well, both verbally and in writing. Understands nonverbal communication and listens effectively.

Beyond presenting information and leading discussions, it is vital for a facilitator to be highly skilled in all aspects of communication. The facilitator should use language that learners can understand; give clear directions for activities; involve trainees through appropriate humor, anecdotes, and examples; and build on the ideas of others. This will lead to training sessions that are engaging and highly valuable for the participants. Facilitators must also be able to listen well and attend to learners' nonverbal communication to create common meaning and mutual understanding.

ASSESSMENT 4, continued

Emotional Intelligence
Respects learners' viewpoints, knowledge, and experience. Recognizes and responds appropriately to others' feelings, attitudes, and concerns.

Because learners may have many different backgrounds, experience levels, and opinions in the same training sessions, facilitators must be able to handle a variety of situations and conversations well and be sensitive to others' emotions. They must pay close attention to the dynamics in the room, be flexible enough to make immediate changes to activities during training to meet the needs of learners, and create an open and trusting learning environment. Attendees should feel comfortable expressing their opinions, asking questions, and participating in activities without fear of repercussion or disapproval. Monitoring learners' emotions during a training session also helps the facilitator gauge when it may be time to change gears if conflict arises, if discussion needs to be refocused on desired outcomes, or if there is a need to delve deeper into a topic to encourage further learning.

Training Methods
Varies instructional approaches to hold learners' interest.

An effective facilitator must be familiar with a variety of training methods to tap into each participant's style and maintain interest during the training session. These methods may include such activities as small group activities, individual exercises, case studies, role plays, simulations, and games.

Subject Matter Expertise
Possesses deep knowledge of training content and applicable experience to draw upon.

Facilitators must have solid background knowledge of the training topic and be able to share related experiences to help learners connect theory to real-world scenarios. Anecdotes and other examples to illustrate how the training content relates to participants' circumstances and work can enhance the learning experience and encourage learners to apply the information. This will also help them use the tools they have been given. It is also crucial that facilitators know their topics inside and out, so they can

---

ASSESSMENT 4, continued

answer the trainees' questions and guide them toward problem solving and skill development.

Questioning Skills
Asks questions in a way that stimulates learners' understanding and curiosity. Encourages critical thinking.

An effective questioning technique works well to assess learners' understanding of training content. It also provides opportunities for them to analyze information and think critically. When learners ask questions, the facilitator is able to see where there may be confusion or a need to review concepts for better understanding. Similarly, when a facilitator asks thought-provoking questions in a way that invites participation, learners can brainstorm solutions to problems or think about situations to help them apply the training content to the issues they deal with on a regular basis.

Eliciting Behavior Change
Influences others effectively both individually and within groups. Gains support and commitment from others to achieve common goals and desired outcomes.

This competency is important in two ways. First, facilitators must be able to persuade trainees to consider points of view that will lead to desired changes in behavior. Facilitators are often called upon to sell an organization's culture or policies, or to gain learners' participation to achieve the desired results of the training. To do this, facilitators must be able to show that although they respect the trainees' views, the trainees must understand and accept the organization's realities and practices.

Second, effective facilitators must know how to form small groups and work well with them to accomplish tasks, work through problems, and fulfill the needs of the group members. Drawing out a group's creative energy through brainstorming or other activities, as well as helping group members blend their knowledge and skills to achieve a common goal, will lead to greater commitment on behalf of the learners to improve their behavior and apply the training content.

Assessment 4, *continued*

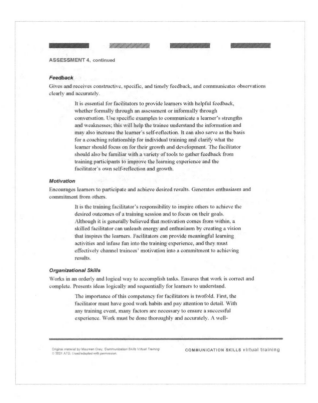

ASSESSMENT 4, continued

Feedback
Gives and receives constructive, specific, and timely feedback, and communicates observations clearly and accurately.

It is essential for facilitators to provide learners with helpful feedback, whether formally through an assessment or informally through conversation. Use specific examples to communicate a learner's strengths and weaknesses; this will help the trainee understand the information and may also increase the learner's self-reflection. It can also serve as the basis for a coaching relationship for individual training and clarify what the learner should focus on for their growth and development. The facilitator should also be familiar with a variety of tools to gather feedback from training participants to improve the learning experience and the facilitator's own self-reflection and growth.

Motivation
Encourages learners to participate and achieve desired results. Generates enthusiasm and commitment from others.

It is the training facilitator's responsibility to inspire others to achieve the desired outcomes of a training session and to focus on their goals. Although it is generally believed that motivation comes from within, a skilled facilitator can unleash energy and enthusiasm by creating a vision that inspires the learners. Facilitators can provide meaningful learning activities and infuse fun into the training experience, and they must effectively channel trainees' motivation into a commitment to achieving results.

Organizational Skills
Works in an orderly and logical way to accomplish tasks. Ensures that work is correct and complete. Presents ideas logically and sequentially for learners to understand.

The importance of this competency for facilitators is twofold. First, the facilitator must have good work habits and pay attention to detail. With any training event, many factors are necessary to ensure a successful experience. Work must be done thoroughly and accurately. A well-

---

Assessment 4, *continued*

ASSESSMENT 4, continued

organized training facilitator typically creates well-organized, professional training.

Second, it is important for facilitators to present ideas in a logical, sequential order that allows learners to absorb new content easily and also to be able to retrieve it quickly. This also increases the probability that the learners will use the content. The more organized the facilitator, the better.

Time Management
Plans and uses time effectively. Balances important and urgent tasks and can work on multiple tasks simultaneously.

Facilitators do many things in addition to conducting training sessions. They must also budget their time effectively to address other priorities in their work, including preparing for the training, keeping accurate records, analyzing assessment data, designing new content or activities, and reporting to the client organization. The most competent facilitators are able to multitask and keep the goals of the learners and client organization in view as much as possible. Good time management helps a facilitator keep track of all there is to do during any given day.

Assessment 4, *continued*

ASSESSMENT 4, continued

Facilitator Competencies
Instructions: If using this instrument as a self-assessment, place a ✓ in the box to the right of each of the 12 facilitator competencies that best describes your skill level. If using this form to provide feedback to a facilitator, place a ✓ in the box that best fits their level of competence in each area.

Competency	Expectations				
	None	Little	Some	Adequate	Expert
Understanding adult learners: Uses knowledge of the principles of adult learning when designing and delivering training.	☐	☐	☐	☐	☐
Presentation skills: Presents content clearly to achieve the desired outcomes of the training. Encourages learners to generate their own answers through effectively leading group discussions.	☐	☐	☐	☐	☐
Communication skills: Expresses self well verbally and in writing. Understands nonverbal communication and listens effectively.	☐	☐	☐	☐	☐
Emotional intelligence: Respects learners' viewpoints, knowledge, and experience. Recognizes and responds appropriately to others' feelings, attitudes, and concerns.	☐	☐	☐	☐	☐
Training methods: Varies instructional approaches to hold learners' interest.	☐	☐	☐	☐	☐
Subject matter expertise: Possesses deep knowledge of training content and applicable experience to draw upon.	☐	☐	☐	☐	☐
Questioning skills: Asks questions in a way that stimulates learners' understanding and curiosity. Encourages critical thinking.	☐	☐	☐	☐	☐
Eliciting behavior change: Influences others effectively, both individually and within groups. Gains support and commitment from others to achieve common goals and desired outcomes.	☐	☐	☐	☐	☐
Feedback: Gives and receives constructive, specific, and timely feedback and communicates observations clearly and accurately.	☐	☐	☐	☐	☐
Motivation: Encourages learners to participate and achieve desired results. Generates enthusiasm and commitment from others.	☐	☐	☐	☐	☐
Organizational skills: Works in an orderly and logical way to accomplish tasks. Ensures work is correct and complete. Presents ideas logically and sequentially for learners to understand.	☐	☐	☐	☐	☐
Time management: Plans time effectively. Balances important and urgent tasks and can work on multiple tasks simultaneously.	☐	☐	☐	☐	☐

Assessment 5: Interpersonal Skills

ASSESSMENT 5

Interpersonal Skills

Instructions: One of the most effective ways to see how your communication skills have improved is to complete the following assessment after you have collaborated in a meeting.

1. How have my reactions and responses changed following the meeting?

2. How will this meeting help me achieve greater professional effectiveness?

3. Do I now have a stronger relationship with that person or people I just met?

4. Do I trust them? Do they trust me?

5. Through collaboration, could we achieve success on both sides of our partnership?

6. What leadership lesson have I learned from this interpersonal exchange?

Assessment 6: Learning Needs Assessment Sheet

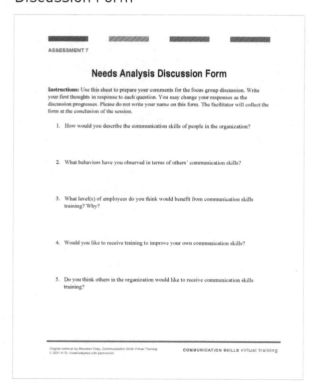

ASSESSMENT 6

Learning Needs Assessment Sheet

Instructions: Use this form to take notes during interviews with stakeholders in the client organization to assess the needs of both learners and the organization itself. Be sure to understand the person's response to each question before you write a summary and assure the interviewee that their comments will be both anonymous and confidential.

1. How do you define communication skills?

2. How would you assess your own communication skills?

3. In your role in the organization, how would you benefit from communication skills training?

4. Would training in communication skills benefit the organization at this time? Why or why not?

5. How would you assess the communication skills of others in the organization?

6. What specific behaviors have you observed regarding organizational skills and productivity that should be addressed in a communication skills course?

7. How do you prefer to receive communication skills training?

8. How interested are others in the organization in receiving communication skills training?

Original material by Maureen Orey, *Communication Skills Virtual Training.*
© 2021 ATD. Used/adapted with permission.
COMMUNICATION SKILLS virtual training

Assessment 6, *continued*

ASSESSMENT 6, continued

9. Should all the employees in the organization receive communication skills training, or only select groups? Why?

10. How should communication skills training be marketed internally to draw attendees?

11. What desired results would you like to see for the organization after communication skills training?

12. What else can you tell me about your training needs at this time?

13. What are other factors for success that could affect communication skills training?

14. What questions do you have for me?

At the end of the interview, thank the person for their candid responses to your questions. Reassure the interviewee that the information will not be quoted by name, just combined with other participants' responses to analyze common themes. Explain that the communication skills training will reflect the priorities of those interviewed.

Original material by Maureen Orey, *Communication Skills Virtual Training.*
© 2021 ATD. Used/adapted with permission.
COMMUNICATION SKILLS virtual training

Assessment 7: Needs Analysis Discussion Form

ASSESSMENT 7

Needs Analysis Discussion Form

Instructions: Use this sheet to prepare your comments for the focus group discussion. Write your first thoughts in response to each question. You may change your responses as the discussion progresses. Please do not write your name on this form. The facilitator will collect the form at the conclusion of the session.

1. How would you describe the communication skills of people in the organization?

2. What behaviors have you observed in terms of others' communication skills?

3. What level(s) of employees do you think would benefit from communication skills training? Why?

4. Would you like to receive training to improve your own communication skills?

5. Do you think others in the organization would like to receive communication skills training?

Original material by Maureen Orey, *Communication Skills Virtual Training.*
© 2021 ATD. Used/adapted with permission.
COMMUNICATION SKILLS virtual training

Assessment 7, *continued*

ASSESSMENT 7, continued

6. What challenges or roadblocks may be present in the organization that could affect the success of a communication skills training session?

7. How would you prefer that training be offered to you? (circle one)
    a. Private, individual instruction
    b. Half-day group session
    c. One-day group session
    d. Multi-day group session
    e. No preference

Thank you for your cooperation in this needs analysis.

Original material by Maureen Orey, *Communication Skills Virtual Training.*
© 2021 ATD. Used/adapted with permission.
COMMUNICATION SKILLS virtual training

COMMUNICATION SKILLS virtual training

Assessment 8: Nonverbal Communication Self-Assessment

Assessment 8, *continued*

ASSESSMENT 8, continued

Analysis

The results of this assessment can help direct your focus on areas of improvement as a giver or receiver of nonverbal feedback. You may find that you score higher as a giver than as a receiver, or that you score higher on particular items in either category.

As a giver of nonverbal feedback, if you rated yourself in the "To Some Extent" or "Not at All" areas for items 1, 2, 5, or 6, this means that you should pay particular attention to others' moods, emotions, and circumstances in the interaction and adapt accordingly. If you scored low on items 3, 4, or 7, you may need to try to keep the receiver's interest through your nonverbal communication.

As a receiver of nonverbal feedback, ratings in the "To Some Extent" or "Not at All" areas for items 8–14 indicate a need to be more sensitive to others' nonverbal messages and improve your focus on the meaning of the giver. You may also need to pay attention to your own nonverbal responses and find ways to minimize any negative or defensive behaviors.

Assessment 9: Skills Application Reflection

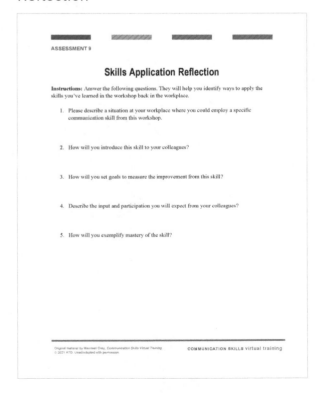

Assessment 10: Skills Mastery Assessment

ASSESSMENT 10

Skills Mastery Assessment

Instructions: Answer the following questions. They will help you assess your communication skills mastery.

1. If you were asked to teach one skill in this workshop, which would it be?

2. What would your three key message points be for that skill?

3. Describe the steps you would take to instruct each message point (for example, lecture, group discussion, PowerPoint presentation).

4. What methods would you use to ensure that your participants understood your instruction?

5. Would feedback from your participants, both positive and negative, affect the development of your skills mastery? If yes, illustrate your response and the changes you would make.

Chapter 12

Handouts

What's in This Chapter

- Twenty-nine handouts in thumbnail format for reference
- Refer to chapter 13 for instructions to download full-size handouts

Handouts comprise the various materials you will provide to the learners throughout the course of the workshop. In some cases, the handouts will simply provide instructions for worksheets to complete, places to take notes, and so forth. In other cases, they will provide important and practical materials for use in and out of the training room, such as reference materials, tip sheets, samples of completed forms, flowcharts, and so forth.

The workshop agendas in chapters 1–3 and the learning activities in chapter 10 will provide instructions for how and when to use the handouts within the context of the workshop. See chapter 13 for complete instructions on how to download the workshop support materials.

Handouts Included in *Communication Skills Virtual Training*

Handout 1a: Objective Decision (Two-Day Workshop)

Handout 1b: Objective Decision (One-Day Workshop)

Handout 1c: Objective Decision (Half-Day Workshop)

Handout 2: The Most Difficult Person in the World

Handout 3: Causes of Miscommunication

Handout 4: The Importance of Body Language

Handout 5: Impression Improv

Handout 1a: Objective Decision (Two-Day Workshop)

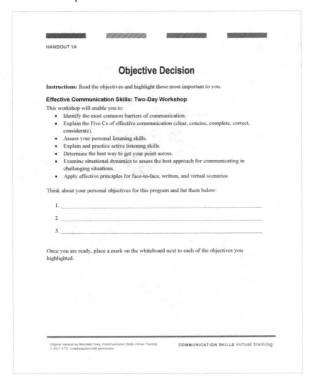

Handout 1b: Objective Decision (One-Day Workshop)

Handout 1c: Objective Decision (Half-Day Workshop)

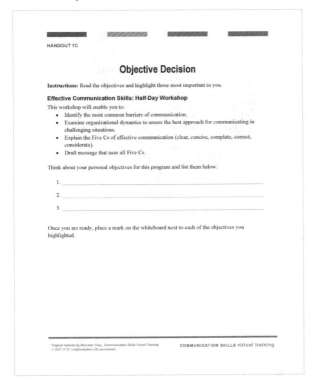

Handout 2: The Most Difficult Person in the World

Handout 3: Causes of Miscommunication

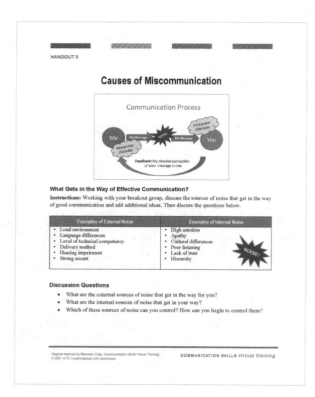

Handout 4: The Importance of Body Language

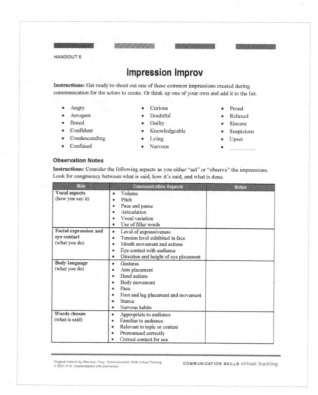

Handout 7: Role of Emotion in Communication

Role of Emotion in Communication

Role of Emotion in Communication

Emotional triggers are things that cause you to react to a situation in an emotional way. These can be events such as someone telling you that you are wrong, lying to you, or being disrespectful. Emotional triggers are different for everyone.

What are the triggers that can cause you to react emotionally?

- _____
- _____
- _____
- _____
- _____

COMMUNICATION SKILLS virtual training

Handout 8: Emotions and the Brain

Emotions and the Brain

Part 1. Roles of the Emotional and Rational Brain

Emotional Brain:

_____

_____

Rational Brain:

_____

_____

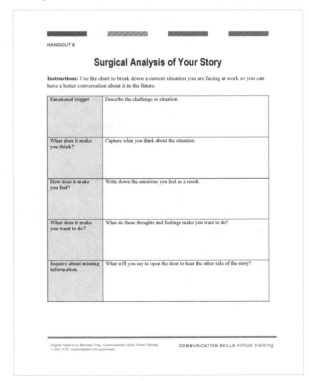

Part 2. Strategies for Gaining Emotional Control

What are your best strategies for gaining control when emotions run high?

_____

_____

_____

_____

_____

_____

_____

COMMUNICATION SKILLS virtual training

Handout 9: Surgical Analysis of Your Story

Surgical Analysis of Your Story

Instructions: Use the chart to break down a current situation you are facing at work so you can have a better conversation about it in the future.

Emotional trigger	Describe the challenge or situation.
What does it make you think?	Capture what you think about the situation.
How does it make you feel?	Write down the emotions you feel as a result.
What does it make you want to do?	What do these thoughts and feelings make you want to do?
Inquire about missing information.	What will you say to open the door to hear the other side of the story?

COMMUNICATION SKILLS virtual training

Handout 10: Mistakes in Listening

Mistakes in Listening

Typical, Nonempathic Listening

- **Listening:** Intending to reply with a solution, opinion, or advice.
- **Filtering:** Screening everything through your own paradigm or agenda.
- **Evaluating:** Determining if you agree or disagree.
- **Probing:** Asking from your frame of reference.
- **Advising:** Giving counsel based on your experience.
- **Interpreting:** Trying to analyze or figure people out.

Notes

_____

_____

_____

_____

_____

_____

_____

COMMUNICATION SKILLS virtual training

Handout 11: Active Listening

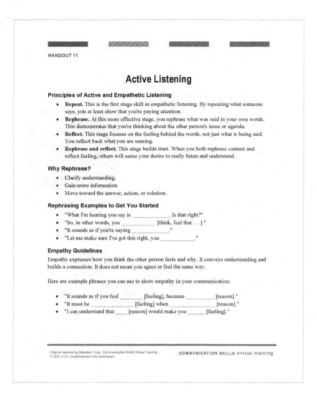

Handout 12: Barriers to Effective Listening

Handout 13: Action Plan and Reflection

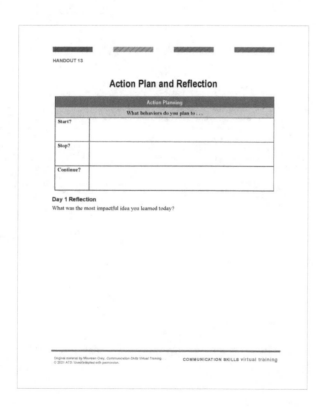

Handout 14: Alpha Beta Exercise

Handout 15: Model for Effective Business Writing

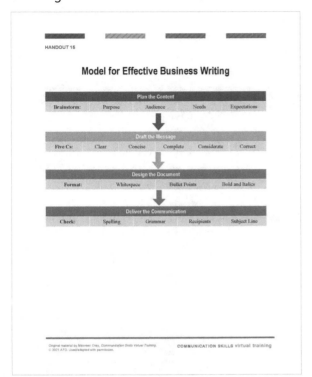

Handout 16: Personal Case Scenario Worksheet

Personal Case Scenario Worksheet

Instructions: Think of recent or current business communication pieces that you can use to review, prepare, or evaluate later in the workshop. Jot down a brief description of the communication and any challenges or difficulties associated with it.

Scenario 1

Scenario 2

Scenario 3

Handout 17: Mind Map: Plan Your Content

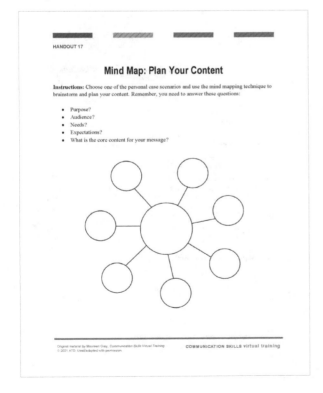

Handout 18: Brainstorm Other Brainstorming Methods

Brainstorm Other Brainstorming Methods

Instructions: Brainstorming can be a very effective tool for planning and strategizing. Practice the technique by brainstorming other brainstorming methods using the guidelines below.

Mind Mapping
- _____
- _____
- _____
- _____
- _____

Brainstorming Guidelines
- Welcome all ideas without judgment.
- Capture all ideas in writing (use the chat window or designated whiteboard so that everyone can see).
- Clarify any ideas that are unclear.
- Pay attention to each other and avoid interruptions.
- Encourage ideas from each participant.
- Narrow the list of options for consideration.
- Prioritize options and decide next steps.
- Try to have fun and be relaxed.

Handout 19: The Five Cs of Effective Communication

The Five Cs of Effective Communication

1. **Clear: Construct Effective Sentences**
   - Create bullets and highlights for key information.
   - Use the right level of language for the audience.
   - Use precise and familiar words.
   - Check your accuracy.

2. **Concise: Eliminate Wordy Expressions**
   - Include only relevant material.
   - Focus on your purpose.
   - Delete anything irrelevant.
   - Avoid lengthy explanations.
   - Avoid unnecessary repetition.

3. **Complete: Provide All Necessary Information**
   - Who
   - What
   - When
   - Where
   - Why
   - How

4. **Correct: Be Sure the Message Is Accurate, Logical, and Orderly**
   - Consider the best order to introduce the information.
   - Check all information and facts for accuracy.
   - Ensure the message's flow and tone are consistent.

5. **Considerate: Put Yourself in Your Reader's Shoes**
   - Focus on the reader instead of yourself.
   - Say "no" by emphasizing what you can do.
   - Apologize when necessary.
   - Use expressions that show respect.
   - Give the reader your complete contact information.

Handout 20: Practical Practice—Clear Communication

Practical Practice—Clear Communication

Instructions: Follow these instructions to practice writing with clarity. Work in pairs so that you can check each other's work.

1. A Martian ship has landed on Earth, and the Martians are here to learn our customs and procedures. The Martians can read English, but they know nothing else about our customs.
2. Your task is to write instructions for a common human task, such as brushing teeth, combing hair, or getting dressed so the Martians can start practicing these healthy human habits.
3. Do your best to include the guidelines for all Five Cs (clear, concise, complete, correct, considerate).
4. Exchange your writing with your partner to check each other's work.
5. Be prepared to share your instructions with the class.

Directions for a Martian (focus on clarity):

_____

_____

_____

_____

_____

_____

_____

_____

Handout 21: Practical Practice—Concise Communication

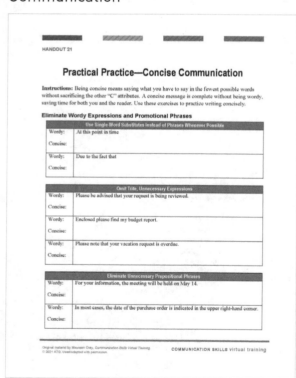

Practical Practice—Concise Communication

Instructions: Being concise means saying what you have to say in the fewest possible words without sacrificing the other "C" attributes. A concise message is complete without being wordy, saving time for both you and the reader. Use these exercises to practice writing concisely.

Eliminate Wordy Expressions and Promotional Phrases

Use Single Word Substitutes Instead of Phrases Whenever Possible	
Wordy:	At this point in time
Concise:	
Wordy:	Due to the fact that
Concise:	

Omit Trite, Unnecessary Expressions	
Wordy:	Please be advised that your request is being reviewed.
Concise:	
Wordy:	Enclosed please find my budget report.
Concise:	
Wordy:	Please note that your vacation request is overdue.
Concise:	

Eliminate Unnecessary Prepositional Phrases	
Wordy:	For your information, the meeting will be held on May 14.
Concise:	
Wordy:	In most cases, the date of the purchase order is indicated in the upper right-hand corner.
Concise:	

Handout 21, _continued_

Omit Promotional Phrases in Response to Complaints	
Wordy:	At ABC Roofing, we place enormous emphasis on our ability to provide exceptional customer service.
Concise:	

Include Only Relevant Material

A concise message should omit not only unnecessary expressions but also irrelevant statements. Keep the following rules in mind:

- Stick to the purpose of the message.
- Delete irrelevant words and rambling sentences.
- Omit information obvious to the receiver; do not repeat at length what the reader already knows.
- Avoid long introductions, unnecessary explanations, excessive adjectives and prepositions, and pompous words.

Avoid Unnecessary Repetition

Sometimes repetition is necessary for emphasis. But when the same thing is said two or three times without reason, the message becomes redundant and boring. Take a look at this example:

> Thank you in advance for attending the conference in Washington, DC, instead of New York as New York is already filled and Washington, DC, has a few seats left. Also, the Washington, DC, fees are less than the New York fees.

How would you fix this message?

_____

_____

_____

_____

Handout 22: Practical Practice— Complete Communication

Practical Practice—Complete Communication

Instructions: Work with a partner to make this email more complete. The trick with this "C" is to provide precise, specific, and needed information without becoming wordy or redundant. Work hard to balance the need for completeness with the principles you learned in the third "C"—concise.

Sample Email

To: All Staff
From: Sam Smith
Subject: Staff Meeting

There will be a mandatory staff meeting tomorrow at 3:00.

Handout 23: Practical Practice— Checklist for Correct Communication

Practical Practice—Checklist for Correct Communication

Instructions: Use this tool to review your documents for completeness.

- ☐ Are all key stakeholders mentioned properly in the document?
- ☐ Are all names and titles spelled correctly?
- ☐ Have the proper dates and times or deadlines been noted accurately?
- ☐ If a location is relevant to this message, has it been noted correctly?
- ☐ Have you tested web links to make sure they send the reader to the correct information?
- ☐ Are all relevant documents attached?
- ☐ If needed, have the appropriate stakeholders signed off on this communication?

Handout 24: Practical Practice—Your Role in Considerate Communication

Practical Practice—Your Role in Considerate Communication

Instructions: Identify the influences in your life that have shaped who you are today. The center of the circle is you, and the surrounding circles are the various life experiences that influenced you—such as your education, geography, religion, family, socioeconomic status, hobbies, and extracurricular activities.

Circles of Influence

Reflection: How can being more aware of your cultural differences, biases, and filters help you be a more considerate communicator?

Handout 25: The Wants and Needs of Your Reader

The Wants and Needs of Your Reader

The Reader Wants	The Reader Needs

Notes

Handout 26: Draft Your Message

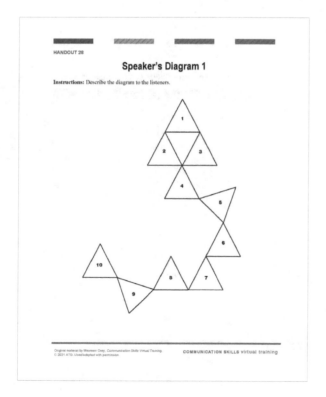

Handout 27: Reflection and Action Plan

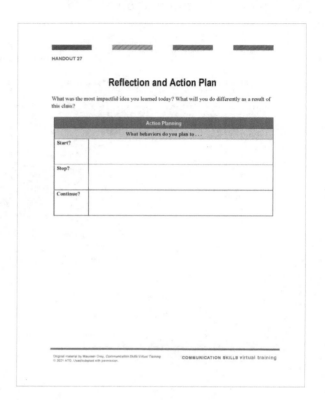

Handout 28: Speaker's Diagram 1

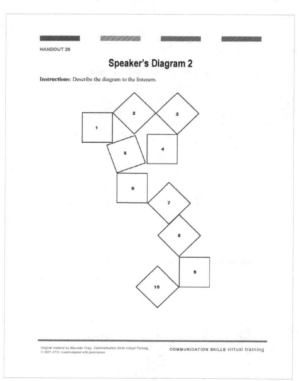

Handout 29: Speaker's Diagram 2

Chapter 13
Online Tools and Downloads

What's in This Chapter

- Instructions to access supporting materials
- Options for using tools and downloads
- Licensing and copyright information for workshop programs
- Tips for working with the downloaded files

The ATD Workshop Series is designed to give you flexible options for many levels of training facilitation and topic expertise. As you prepare your program, you will want to incorporate many of the handouts, assessments, presentation slides, and other training tools provided as supplementary materials with this volume. We wish you the best of luck in delivering your training workshops. It is exciting work that ultimately can change lives.

Access to Free Supporting Materials

To get started, visit the ATD Workshop Series page: td.org/workshopbooks. This page includes links to download all the free supporting materials that accompany this book, as well as up-to-date information about additions to the series and new program offerings.

These downloads, which are included in the price of the book, feature ready-to-use learning activities, handouts, assessments, and presentation slide files in PDF format. Use these files to deliver your workshop program and as a resource to help you prepare your own materials. You may download and use any of these files as part of your training delivery for the workshops, provided no changes are made to the original materials. To access this material, you will be asked to log into the ATD website. If you are not an ATD member, you will have to create an ATD account.

If you choose to recreate these documents, they can only be used within your organization; they cannot be presented or sold as your original work. Please note that all materials included in the book are copyrighted and you are using them with permission of ATD. If you choose to recreate the materials, per copyright usage requirements, you must provide attribution to the original source of the content and display a copyright notice as follows:

© 2021 ATD. Adapted and used with permission.

Customizable Materials

You can also choose to customize this supporting content for an additional licensing fee. This option gives you access to a downloadable zip file with the entire collection of supporting materials in Microsoft Word and PowerPoint file formats. Once purchased, you will have indefinite and unlimited access to these materials through the My Downloads section of your ATD account. Then, you will be able to customize and personalize all the documents and presentations using Microsoft Word and PowerPoint. You can add your own content, change the order or format, include your company logo, or make any other customization.

Please note that all the original documents contain attribution to ATD and this book as the original source for the material. As you customize the documents, remember to keep these attributions intact (see the copyright notice above). By doing so, you are practicing professional courtesy by respecting the intellectual property rights of another trainer (the author) and modeling respect for copyright and intellectual property laws for your program participants.

ATD offers two custom material license options: Internal Use and Client Use. To determine which license option you need to purchase, ask yourself the following question:

Will I or my employer be charging a person or outside organization a fee for providing services or for delivering training that includes any ATD Workshop content that you wish to customize?

If the answer is yes, then you need to purchase a Client Use license.

If the answer is no, and you plan to customize ATD Workshop content to deliver training at no cost to employees within your own department or company only, you need to purchase the Internal Use license.

Working With the Files

PDF Documents

To read or print the PDF files you download, you must have PDF reader software such as Adobe Acrobat Reader installed on your system. The program can be downloaded free of cost from the Adobe website: adobe.com. To print documents, simply use the PDF reader to open the downloaded files and print as many copies as you need.

PowerPoint Slides

To use or adapt the contents of the PowerPoint presentation files (available with the Internal Use and Client Use licenses), you must have Microsoft PowerPoint software installed on your system. If you simply want to view the PowerPoint documents, you only need an appropriate viewer on your system. Microsoft provides various viewers for free download at microsoft.com.

Once you have downloaded the files to your computer system, use Microsoft PowerPoint (or free viewer) to print as many copies of the presentation slides as you need. You can also make handouts of the presentations by choosing the "print three slides per page" option on the print menu.

You can modify or otherwise customize the slides by opening and editing them in Microsoft PowerPoint. However, you must retain the credit line denoting the original source of the material, as noted earlier in this chapter. It is illegal to present this content as your own work. The files will open as read-only files, so before you adapt them you will need to save them onto your hard drive.

The PowerPoint slides included in this volume support the three workshop agendas:

- Two-Day Workshop
- One-Day Workshop
- Half-Day Workshop

For PowerPoint slides to successfully support and augment your learning program, it is essential that you practice giving presentations with the slides *before* using them in live training situations. You should be confident that you can logically expand on the points featured in the presentations and discuss the methods for working through them. If you want to fully engage your participants, become familiar with this technology before you use it. See the text box that follows for a cheat sheet to help you navigate through the presentation. A good practice is to insert comments into PowerPoint's notes feature, which you can print out and use when you present the slides. The workshop agendas in this book show thumbnails of each slide to help you keep your place as you deliver the workshop.

NAVIGATING THROUGH A POWERPOINT PRESENTATION	
Key	**PowerPoint "Show" Action**
Space bar or Enter or mouse click	Advance through custom animations embedded in the presentation
Backspace	Back up to the last projected element of the presentation
Escape	Abort the presentation
B or b	Blank the screen to black
B or b (repeat)	Resume the presentation
W or w	Blank the screen to white
W or w (repeat)	Resume the presentation

Distributing Materials to Participants

When delivering the workshop in a virtual environment, it will be important to provide participants with electronic copies of any materials they will need to print in advance of the course. You may compile the .pdf versions of the necessary files and send them via email or through a file sharing service such as OneDrive, DropBox, or Google Docs.

Again, all materials included in the book are copyrighted and you are using them with permission of ATD. If you choose to recreate the materials, per copyright usage requirements, you must provide attribution to the original source of the content and display a copyright notice as follows:

© 2021 ATD. Adapted and used with permission.

Acknowledgments

I can't help but think of the old saying that it takes a village to raise a child; in many ways this book was not written by me alone. Without the support of my friends, family, and colleagues this book would have taken an eternity to complete. Many thanks to my intern, Debby Tang, from the University of California, San Diego—your keen eye for detail and friendly disposition never failed, and your willingness and patience to deal with my crazy travel schedule was truly a lifesaver! Thanks also to the fabulous learning leaders and contributing authors—Rick Hicks, Dawn Mahoney, and Sharon Wingron. The ideas and activities you provided have added to the quality and strength of this book. Special thanks particularly to Ken Phillips who not only shared a great learning activity but also the Communication Style Inventory—one of the most spectacular resources in the book!

Of course, I would be remiss not to mention the team at ATD Press—especially Melissa Jones, her work is spot on and always professional! Cat Russo originally championed the updated workshop series, editor Jacki Edlund-Braun kept nudging me gently as deadlines loomed, and Tora Estep was brilliant with her insights. Thank you for all your gracious support as the original work was completed.

As always, without fail, my friends and family always had nothing but love and support for me. Thank you Vey for keeping me fed, loved, and sane during the long days; Shane, Danielle, and Rachel I appreciate your inspiration and understanding.

I am blessed beyond belief to have this village of support—my deepest thanks to all.

About the Author

 **Maureen C. Orey** is an award-winning international speaker, expert facilitator, and executive coach with more than two decades of experience in the fields of communication, resilience, leadership, training, diversity, and inclusion. She has worked in many industries, including technology, healthcare, construction, hospitality, and education. Her client list includes Boeing, Sony Corp, Scripps Health, SHARP Healthcare, San Diego State University, the Scaffold Industry Association, the Association for Talent Development, the City of San Diego, the US Marine Corps, and the US Navy. As the founder and CEO of the Workplace Learning & Performance Group, Maureen is dedicated to working with inspired individuals and organizations to build their resilience through effective communication, diverse teams, and inclusive leadership strategies.

Maureen is co-author of the bestselling *Communication Skills Training* (ASTD Press 2004; ATD Press 2014), *A Year of Resilience* (Stay Afloat Press 2020), and *Successful Staffing* in a Diverse Workplace (Richard Chang Associates). She is a Certified Professional in Talent Development (CPTD), holds a doctorate in organizational leadership, a master's in education from the University of San Diego, and a bachelor's degree in psychology from San Diego State University. In addition to her work in the private sector, she currently serves as adjunct professor at University of California, San Diego, teaching courses on leading and managing change.

Among her many professional recognitions, Maureen was honored with the ATD 2017 Dissertation of the Year award for her research on the career benefits and ROI of volunteer leadership. She has been recognized as an outstanding Instructor of the Year for San Diego State University's College of Extended Studies and her company, the Workplace Learning & Performance Group, is proud to be the winner of the San Diego Regional Chamber of Commerce's Small Business Awards.

Maureen is passionate about resilience, balance, and embracing the differences that make us strong. Originally from San Diego, she is a proud mother of three children and enjoys sipping a nice red wine and staying afloat on her boat in Coronado, California.

Contact Maureen via email (Maureen@wlpgroup.com), phone (619.475.8397), the web (wlpgroup.com), Twitter (@trainingleader), Facebook (Maureen Orey or Workplace Learning & Performance Group), or LinkedIn (linkedin.com/in/maureenorey).

About ATD

The Association for Talent Development (ATD) is the world's largest professional membership organization supporting those who develop the knowledge and skills of employees, improve performance, and achieve results for the organizations they serve. Originally established in 1943, the association was previously known as the American Society for Training & Development (ASTD).

ATD's members come from more than 120 countries and work in public and private organizations in every industry sector. ATD supports talent development professionals who gather locally in volunteer-led U.S. chapters and international member networks, and with international strategic partners. For more information, visit td.org.

1640 King Street
Alexandria, VA 22314
www.td.org
800.628.2783
703.683.8100